LEADER'S GUIDE • REPRODUCIBLE PAGES

CONNECT

LIFE & CHRISTIAN FAITH FOR YOUNG TEENS

VOLUME 3

TABLE OF C-O-N-T

CONNECT

·E·N·T·S

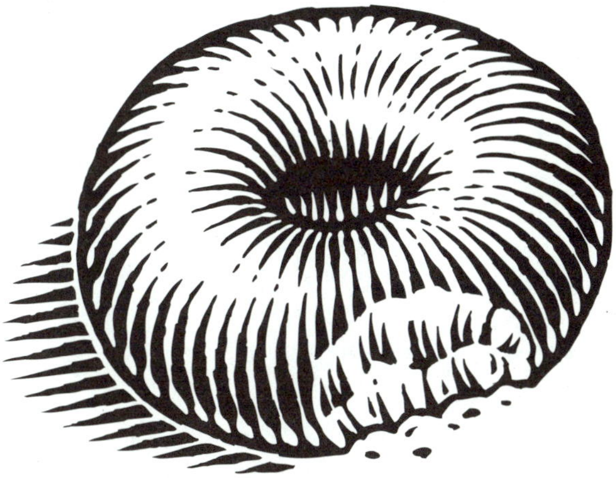

CONNECT Life and Christian Faith for Young Teens
Volume 3 (ISSN 1086-8593)

Printed in the United States of America.

This book is printed on recycled, acid-free paper.

Scripture quotations in this publication, unless otherwise indicated, are from the *New Revised Standard Version Bible*, copyright © 1989 by the Division of Christian Education of the National Council of the Churches of Christ in the United States of America. Used by permission.

To order copies of this publication, call 1-800-672-1789. Call Monday-Friday, 7:00-6:30 Central Time; 5:00-4:30 Pacific Time; Saturday, 9:00-5:00. Telecommunication Device for the Deaf/Telex Telephone: 800-227-4091. Automated order system is available after office hours. Use your Cokesbury account, American Express, Visa, Discover, or MasterCard.

EDITORIAL AND DESIGN TEAM
M. Steven Games, Ron R. Robinson, *Editors*
Carol B. Atkins, *Assistant Editor*
Phillip Francis, *Design Supervisor*
Diana K. Maio, *Designer*

ADMINISTRATIVE TEAM
Neil M. Alexander, *Publisher*
Duane A. Ewers, *Editor of Church School Publications*
M. Steven Games, *Senior Editor of Youth Publications*

Cover by FPG International

96 97 98 99 00 01 02 03 04 05—10 9 8 7 6 5 4 3 2 1

Abingdon Press

WHAT IS CONNECT?

HOW CAN WE BE A POSITIVE INFLUENCE IN THE LIFE OF YOUTH?
HOW DO WE KEEP YOUTH INVOLVED IN THE LIFE OF THE CHURCH?
HOW DO WE HELP THEM GROW IN FAITH?

CONNECT will help you deal with these concerns by connecting with younger adolescents at the level of their basic life issues and needs.

The connections are based on a combination of:

1. the developmental needs of early adolescents
2. key elements in the Bible and Christian faith
3. tying Bible and faith to life

Part of the process of developing **CONNECT** was to give youth from all over the nation a list of topics and to ask:

➤ What are the questions you have about this topic?

➤ What are your issues?

We asked them to be blunt and honest and to push the edges. Our writers used these questions in developing the units and sessions. So you have material for dealing with real life concerns from real youth, not something dreamed up somewhere.

CONNECT OFFERS

➤ reproducible student pages

➤ a balance of short, lively units on Bible, life, and faith

➤ a 1-2-3 teaching plan with plenty of options

➤ activities that will appeal to various learning styles

➤ a session-at-a-glance chart

➤ last minute, easy preparation options for substitute teachers

➤ bonus pages for parents, worship planners, broadly-graded classes

➤ perforated pages

WHAT'S IN A UNIT?

TITLE PAGE

shows the unit title and the session titles; offers a brief purpose statement about that topic.

This Is Not Junk Mail!

may be duplicated and given to parents, guardians, and other interested adults so that they:

- know what the unit is about and know how they can encourage or participate in conversations about the topic at home.
- understand the importance of the topic for youth and understand tough questions or realities that youth face about the topic.
- discover ways to incorporate the topic into family activities.
- become more familiar with young adolescent developmental issues.

Hallelujah!

offers suggestions for worship in the class setting. Hallelujah! can be duplicated and given to the pastor, choir director, and members of the worship work area in your congregation. Folks can use the worship materials and ideas to help make worship more "youth friendly."

Miscellany

is designed to help teachers who have both middle schoolers and high school youth in the same class. Miscellany gives tips on how to use the unit material with a wide age range, suggestions for special activities and projects, or ideas for intergenerational activities.

Following these unit pages will be session plans for one to three sessions.

WHAT'S IN A SESSION PLAN?

Each session has a specific lesson plan, with options.

Read Me

includes Bible background, material on the teachings of the church, background on the issue or topic, statistical information, developmental background on younger adolescents, and questions youth have about the topic. Read the Read Me page(s) in preparation for every session.

???

also known as the YouthPage, may be duplicated and given to youth. In most sessions, this includes activities related to one or more of the options in the lesson plan.

There are five connections in each session.
They are:

Initial **CONNECTION**

CONNECT with the Session

CONNECT with the Bible and the Faith Community

CONNECT with Life

Closing **CONNECTION**

YOU ARE IMPORTANT

Younger adolescents need positive relationships with adults. Positive social interaction with adults and peers is extremely important to young adolescents, and you have an opportunity to play an important part in their lives. You will facilitate a group experience from which youth may establish friendships, self-identity, and faith. Youth need someone who will establish appropriate boundaries and allow them to discover who they are becoming, allow them to belong to a caring community, and allow them to explore and establish their beliefs.

That person is **YOU!**

WHO ARE MY YOUTH?

A major research project conducted for The United Methodist Publishing House showed that, in every class, there are basically three kinds of youth.

55% of the youth surveyed are most interested in

- faith and relationship to God;
- tying the Bible to today's issues;
- learning about the Bible.

30% of the youth surveyed are most interested in

- belonging;
- a safe place to ask tough questions;
- current events (personal);
- helping others;
- informal talk and music.

14% of the youth surveyed are interested in:

- faith and relationship with God;
- current issues, such as environment, racism, poverty.

One of the keys to an involved class is a variety of activities, with some that appeal to each of these three groups.

HOW DO I SELECT ACTIVITIES FOR MY CLASS?

Each learning activity is designed to achieve a Desired Result. For each Desired Result, choose the option most suited to your class. Try to choose options that will appeal to the youth in your class. If you have more than 45 minutes, you may want to select additional options.

As you "customize" your session, be sure you consider activities that are active and experiential, as well as some that involve discussion and reflection. Be sure to open your class with an activity that gets the attention of the youth. This will help them be receptive to the remainder of the activities. Bringing your class session to an appropriate close is also important. The Closing Connection offers an activity for this. You may also want to use some suggestions from the Hallelujah! page to open or close each session.

IF YOU ARE A SUBSTITUTE LOOK FOR THIS ICON
beside the learning activities in each session. These activities can be done with a minimum of preparation and traditional supplies.

MINI-WORKSHOP

BY RON ROBINSON
THE CIRCLE OF LIFE:
BELIEFS, FEELINGS, ACTIONS AND EVENTS

CONNECT WITH THE PARTICIPANTS

5-10 minutes

Have chairs arranged in a semicircle facing the front of the room. You will need newsprint or a chalk/dry erase board and markers or chalk. Having refreshments available would be a good touch. Offer the refreshments during the break time.

WELCOME THE PARTICIPANTS TO THE WORKSHOP.

➤ **Introduce yourself.**

➤ **Ask the participants to introduce themselves.**

➤ **If you have participated in previous workshops in this series, you may want to ask the group if they have been able to apply any of the things they learned in the last workshop.**

CONNECT WITH THE TOPIC

5 minutes

Ahead of time, gather a couple of newspaper articles about adolescents. One should be a story of some negative behavior. Another should be a story of positive teen behavior.

SAY:

➤ **Today we are going to make some important discoveries regarding the beliefs and behaviors of early adolescents. Have you ever wondered why some adolescents seem to live positive lives while others live lives that seem negative? Have you ever wondered why teens respond to situations the way they do? (Review the articles which you have clipped.)**

SAY:

➤ **Today we are going to look at teen behavior. In order to do that, it is important for us to review teens as total people who have individual beliefs, feelings, and actions.**

2 minutes

CONNECT WITH THE BIBLE AND THE COMMUNITY OF FAITH

SAY:

➤ **During his ministry, Jesus demonstrated concern for the total person. If someone was ill, he offered healing. If a person was feeling worthless, he lifted their spirits. If their beliefs were suspect, he challenged them. Jesus understood that our beliefs, emotions and actions are intricately connected. This is true for all people, including young adolescents. Jesus wanted his followers to look beyond the surface in order that they might see deeper things. He spoke to them in parables but urged them to look beyond the simple story in order that they might grasp deeper meaning.**

➤ **Read Matthew 13:10-17 to the group.**

SAY:

➤ **Today we seek to see and hear in a new way. Today we will try to understand with our hearts.**

25 minutes

CONNECT WITH LIFE

A. INTRODUCE THE CIRCLE OF LIFE

At the top of the chalkboard or newsprint write: "Life Is Difficult."

SAY:

➤ **"Life is difficult." Scott Peck begins his bestseller, *The Road Less Traveled,* with these truthful words. Each of us faces a variety of circumstances which evoke reactions from us. Why do people, and adolescents in particular, act the ways they do?**

Let's explore this mystery.

On the board or newsprint write the word **EVENT.**

SAY:

➤ **An event occurs in the life of an adolescent.**

SAY:

➤ **Events never happen in isolation. They are connected to Emotions, Beliefs and Actions. (Write each word on the board as you say it. Your board/newsprint should look like this:**

EVENT

ACTION BELIEF

EMOTION

SAY:

➤ **Each part of this circle is connected to the next part. Let's call this the Circle of Life.**

Draw arrows connecting the circle.

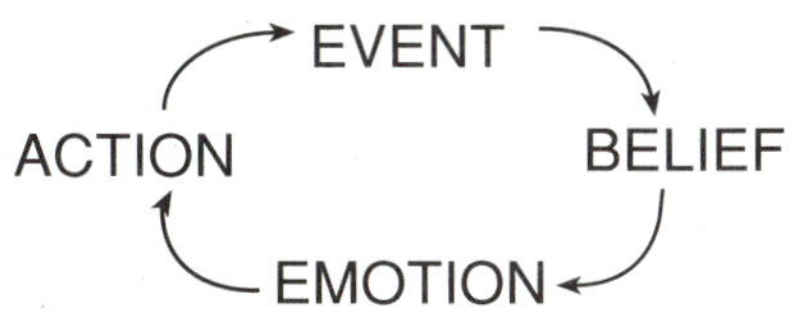

SAY:

➤ **It is important to note two things about the Circle of Life:**

1) **A person may enter it at any point, and** (Draw an arrow coming into each part of the circle.)

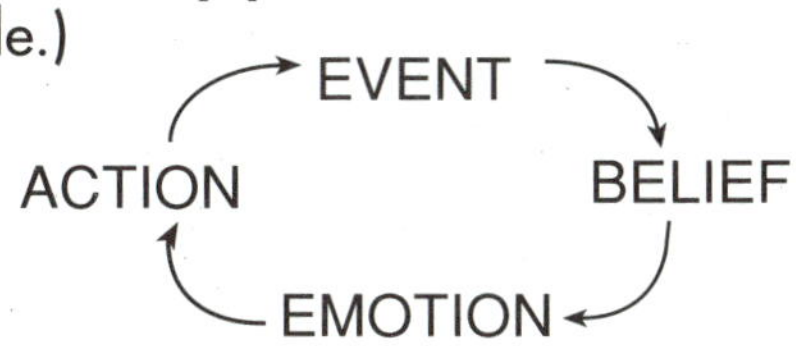

2) **The circle may be either positive or negative.** (Draw a + sign and a - sign.)

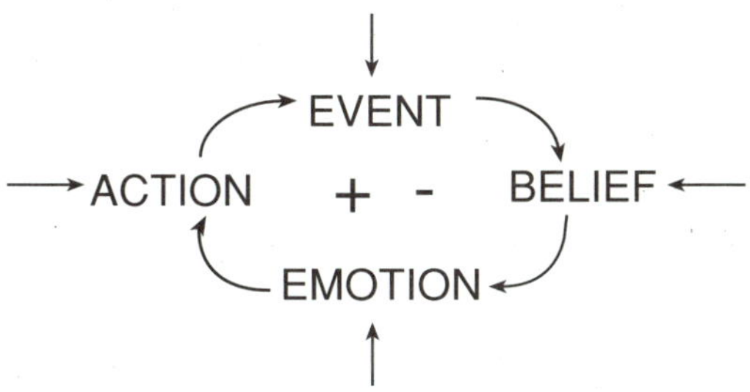

B. THE POSITIVE CIRCLE

Have a Circle of Life on newsprint or on a chalkboard. As you lead the participants through this exercise, write their responses under the appropriate headings.

SAY:

➤ **Now let's take a look at a positive Circle of Life. Let's enter the Circle at the Belief stage. If a young person *believes* himself or herself to be a likable and capable person, then what emotions might they feel?** (*hope, courage, confidence, happiness*)

➤ **If they feel these positive emotions, then what are some likely actions? (Examples: responsible, agreeable, creative, cooperative.) Following such actions, what event might occur?** (*affirmation, praise, encouragement, reward*) **Following such an event, what is a young person likely to believe about himself or herself?** (*likable, capable, high self-esteem*) **What emotions might they experience?** (*hope, courage, confidence, happiness*)

Do you see how the circle keeps repeating itself?

C. THE NEGATIVE CIRCLE

Have another Circle of Life on newsprint or on a chalkboard. Again, as you lead the participants through this exercise, write their responses under the appropriate headings.

SAY:

➤ **Now let's take a look at a negative Circle of Life. Let's enter the Circle at the Belief Stage. If a young person *believes* himself or herself to be an unlikable and unimportant person, then what emotions might he or she feel?** (*worthlessness, discouragement, anger, sadness*)

-**If he or she feels these emotions, then what are some likely actions?** (*irresponsibility, disagreeableness, defiance*)
-**Following such actions, what events might occur?** (*scolding, punishment, withholding of affection, limiting freedoms*)
-**Following such an event, what is a young person likely to believe about himself or herself?** (*unlikable and unimportant*)
-**What emotions might he or she experience?** (*worthlessness, discouragement, anger, sadness*)

Once again, do you see how the Circle of Life keeps repeating itself?

D. MULTIPLE CIRCLES

SAY:

➤ **Young adolescents experience multiple circles in their lives. Some of them include:**

Parents | Peers | Media Influences | Siblings
Bio-Chemical Makeup | Interest Groups | Significant Adults
Authority Figures

As you write these on the chalkboard or newsprint, draw circles around them. Invite the group to suggest others. Remind the group that one youth may experience a circle as positive while another may experience it as negative. Further, not all circles carry the same amount of influence.

If you have refreshments available, this would be a good time for a break.

CONNECT WITH SKILLS

Hand out a copy of the Adolescent Circles of Life Worksheet to each workshop participant. Make certain that everyone has a pen or pencil. Give the following instructions:

SAY:

➤ **You have been given an Adolescent Circles of Life Worksheet. At the top of the sheet, identify several of the circles that impact your adolescent.**

Following that, list the circles in the grid on the bottom half of the sheet. Identify the Beliefs, Emotions, Actions, and Events of each circle. Then determine if it is positive or negative. If it is negative, reflect upon what might be done to transform it to a positive circle. If it is positive, celebrate the good things and determine ways this circle might have an even greater positive impact upon your adolescent.

Allow at least ten minutes for this exercise. Ask if anyone would like to discuss one or more of their circles with the group. Solicit group feedback and encourage them to offer helpful responses. There may be a tendency to complain about certain circles without offering positive suggestions for transformation. Some very direct questions may be appropriate at this point. Questions may include: What do you want for your youth? How can that be achieved? What can you do to influence them? Are you willing to do that?

Remind adults that their degree of influence with their adolescent may range between 0% - 99%. They can never completely control their child. In fact, that would not be healthy. They might be encouraged to discuss ways to increase or lessen their influence.

CLOSING CONNECTION

At this time, it may be appropriate to hand out information concerning upcoming youth activities and events. You may even take time to respond to questions concerning scheduling or youth ministry policies or concerns in your congregation.

SAY:

➤ **Thank you for coming today. I hope this workshop has been helpful and that you will be able to take some skills home with you. Let us conclude our time together with a prayer.**

Conclude with the prayer at right or another of your choosing.

Thank you, God, for that exciting, frightening time of life called adolescence. Thank you for those who love their adolescents and want to understand them and make life better for them.

Let us go from here with new eyes and ears, so that we may see and hear more deeply.

Let us offer love and understanding from the depths of our hearts. We thank you for loving us, and we realize that in your eyes we must seem like adolescents, too; in the love of Christ we pray. Amen.

ADOLESCENT CIRCLES OF LIFE WORKSHEET

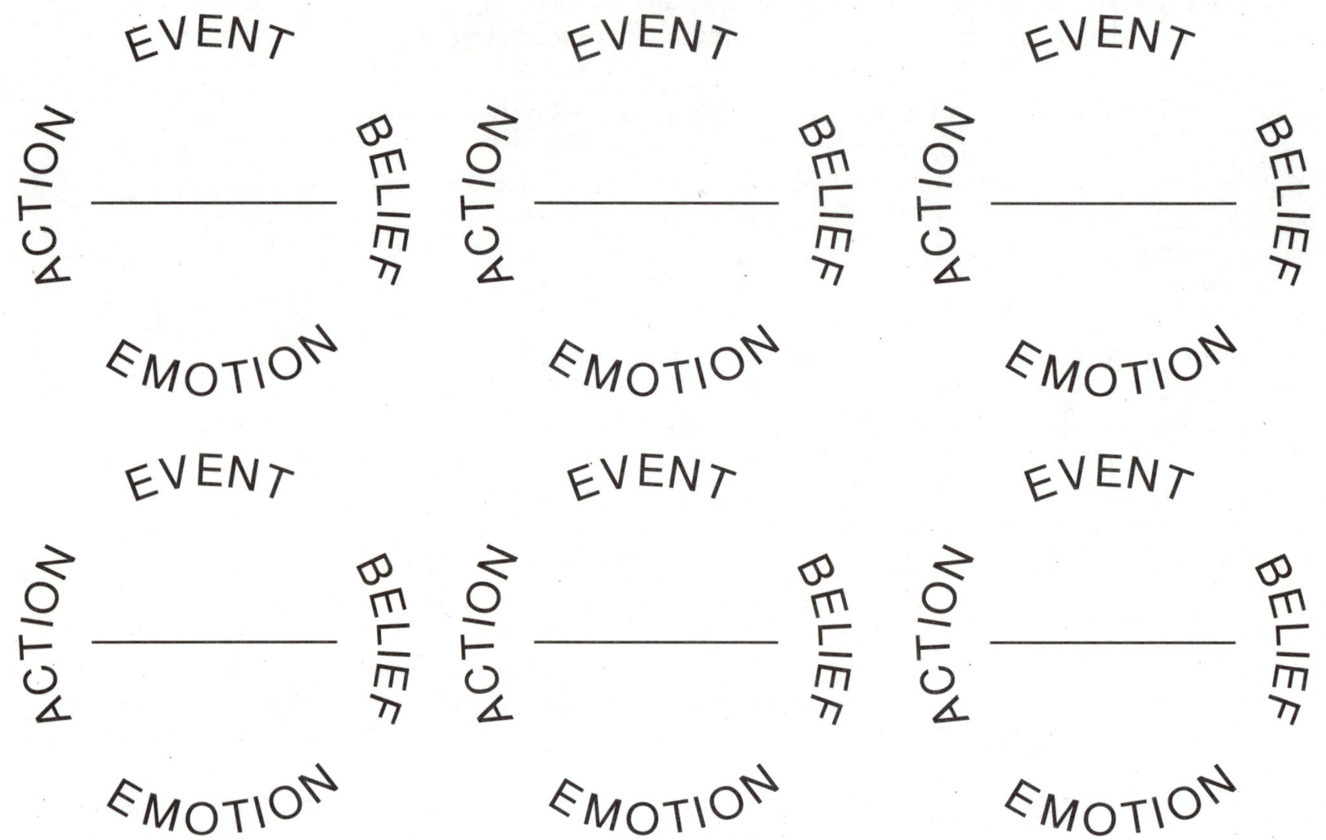

CIRCLE	BELIEFS	EMOTIONS	ACTIONS	EVENTS	+ OR -	CHANGES TO MAKE

TALKIN' THE WALK

© CLEO FREELANCE PHOTOGRAPHY

SESSION 1: SAY, WHAT?

SESSION 2: I CAN'T GET NO . . . SATISFACTION (YES, YOU CAN).

SESSION 3: GETTIN' A GRIP ON IT

Purpose

In this unit youth will practice listening, assertiveness, and conflict resolution skills and will consider how being a good communicator helps them in their Christian "walk."

This Is Not Junk Mail!

IT'S IMPORTANT STUFF FROM YOUR TEENAGER'S SUNDAY MORNING LEADER

THEME TALK

Teenagers, like adults, are frustrated by breakdowns in communication. They may feel ignored, not listened to, or misunderstood. Their personal space may not be respected by others. They may experience undesirable outcomes from not dealing well with conflict. Teenagers can be overwhelmed by their emotions at this developmental phase of their lives, acting out behaviors based on emotion rather than reason. They are usually not pleased with the consequences of those behaviors.

One of the best ways for youth to develop effective communication skills that will bring them more success in relationships, work, and other pursuits is for them to observe those skills being used at home.

POINTERS FOR PARENTS

Your teenager will be studying these skills in this unit. Practice them at home, together.

LISTEN ACTIVELY. Use eye contact and other body language to show attentiveness. Stop what you're doing to listen; limit distractions. Speak **only** to communicate understanding and empathy.

ACT ASSERTIVELY. State feelings, needs, and opinions honestly, but in ways that do not insult or put down others.

KEEP EMOTIONS OUT OF ARGUMENTS. Treat the other person with respect. State your position clearly and restate the other sides position to make sure you understand.

Faith FOCUS

When we communicate well with others, we treat them with respect, understand their needs, and act in loving and supportive ways. Communication helps bind us together as God's people—enabling us to love and nurture each other.

Teenagers need to know that God wants to communicate with them and be in relationship with them. Adults in the faith community can give expression to this desire of God's when they reach out to youth, treat them with respect, and listen to them. They also can help youth deal with conflict, reassuring them that conflict and the accompanying emotions are natural, but that as Christians we are called to handle conflict in ways that respect ourselves and others.

LET'S LISTEN TO OUR CHILDREN

. . . when we get into a listening mode, let's explore our kids' perceptions about their reality. Let's not tell them how to feel or how things ought to be . . . let's just listen. Listening and healing go hand in hand. Let's really listen. People who feel listened to will feel significant, which leads to a feeling that they are being taken seriously and sincerely loved. Once that happens, they believe "I have self-worth." A parent's way of thinking, seeing, and feeling is not the only way. Understanding doesn't mean agreeing, and acceptance is not necessarily approval, but both agreeing and accepting will lead to a sense of rapport, intimacy, and love.

(From *Making Sense of Adolescence*, by John Crudele and Richard Erickson, Triumph Books, 1995; page 200.)

Hallelujah!

IDEAS FOR PEOPLE WHO PLAN WORSHIP

children's SERMON

If your church has a children's sermon or Children's Church time, let youth prepare and lead this. They will need to consider good communication skills when choosing a lesson and their methods for teaching it. They'll need to think of ways to get and maintain the children's attention, speak on their level, and make the lesson relevant and meaningful to a child. Encourage youth to actively involve the children through their senses—seeing (visual props), hearing (music, singing, noises), smelling, touching, and even tasting. Youth might also try to think of a small item to give the children to take home as a reminder of the lesson.

BODY LANGUAGE

"Signing" In

At the beginning of the service, have one or more youth show the congregation how to say "Amen" (or "pray") in sign language. They should then ask the congregation to sign "amen" whenever the word is said during the service.

To sign "amen": Bend elbows, with hands held about six inches apart. Bring palms together and draw hands toward chest, slightly bowing head.

RESPONSIVE READING

Ask youth to select a psalm, or portion of a psalm, which they like and turn it into a responsive reading for worship. Have them choose from a Bible translation which they find easy to read and understand. Next, have them choose certain groups in the congregation to read different verses of the psalm (older adults, youth and children, young adults, males or females). The ending of the psalm, or a repeated verse, could be read together by all.

WORSHIP • MUSIC

Consider ordering a tape or CD of *Youth Praise 3,* and check your hymnal to locate one or more of the following songs for use in worship. Use your youth choir, teenage soloists, chancel choir, or the entire congregation. For a more powerful effect, use a combination of choir(s) and congregation singing different verses or separate parts. Consider using guitars and other instruments for accompaniment. (And don't let the hymns drag; keep them moving!)

"Psalm 71," or "You Make Your Home in Me," (from *Youth Praise 3* CD/cassette available from Cokesbury)
"Help Us Accept Each Other"
"Here I Am, Lord"
"Thy Word Is a Lamp"

Miscellany

IDEAS FOR TEACHERS

YOUNGER YOUTH

Younger youth can be very self-conscious and easily embarrassed around peers, especially when older youth are present. Do not ask younger youth to answer direct questions or to do role-plays in front of the group unless they volunteer.

When asking younger youth to share personal experiences or feelings, you may want to phrase the question in general terms so the attention is somewhat deflected from them. Instead of, "Michael, what do you and your parents argue about?" ask, "What do teenagers argue about with their parents?"

Younger youth are more physically active than older youth and typically have shorter attention spans. Learning activities should involve them physically whenever possible. Avoid lectures or lengthy discussions. Keep the lesson focused and moving, or younger youth (older youth, too) may become distracted and lose interest.

OLDER YOUTH

Younger youth will be watching and listening to the older youth. Take advantage of this by encouraging older youth to participate as much as possible during the lesson.

Older youth tend to be more self-confident and less intimidated than younger adolescents. Ask older youth to act out the role-plays on communication skills. Have them facilitate groups of younger youth during small group activities. Use them as models when demonstrating the listening, assertiveness, and conflict resolution skills covered in this unit.

Older youth have more life experiences in the area of interpersonal communication. Encourage them to share their experiences during discussion activities. Their closeness in age to the younger youth will make them credible and influential contributors.

Outside of class, tell your older youth how important they are as models to the younger ones. Be appreciative of their help and class participation. Ask older youth for their input on how to make the class or a certain topic more meaningful to younger youth, yet still be interesting and helpful to the older ones.

SESSION 1:
SAY, WHAT?

Focus

To help youth develop active listening skills.

Scripture

Psalm 116:1-2

HERE'S THE PLAN **DO IT YOUR WAY**

OPTIONS	TIME (minutes)	PREPARATION	SUPPLIES
INITIAL CONNECTION			
A Burger Bonanza	5–10		
CONNECT WITH THE SESSION			
A Hearing Isn't Listening	10–15		2 chairs, small desk, chalkboard and chalk or dry eraser board and marker
B Listen Up, Partner	10–15	list poor listening habits under the heading "Not Tuned In" on chalkboard or dry eraser board	chalk or marker
CONNECT WITH THE BIBLE AND THE FAITH COMMUNITY			
A God Listens to Me?	10	obtain tape or use substitute song; make copies of YouthPage	Bibles, copies of the student page, *Youth Praise 3* (CD or tape, available from Cokesbury), CD or tape player
CONNECT WITH LIFE			
A Hearing Isn't Listening: Part 2	10	make "Stop, Look, and Listen" poster listing active listening skills	Stop, Look, and Listen poster
B Listen Up Partner, —Again	10		
C Huddle Up	10		
CLOSING CONNECTION			
Pray	1		closing prayer

Desired Result:
To create a warm atmosphere, get youth talking, and introduce the topic.

(Allow 5–10 minutes.)

INITIAL CONNECTION

BURGER BONANZA

With everyone seated in a circle, choose one youth to start as the order taker by asking the person on his or her left, "Can I take your order?" The person should answer, "A hamburger." The order taker than asks, "What do you want on it?" The person chooses a topping to go on the burger (ketchup, cheese, chocolate syrup, peanuts, etc.), then says to the next person, "Can I take your order?" That person answers, "A hamburger." When asked what to put on the burger, the person must repeat the first topping before adding his or her own. This goes around the circle, with each youth repeating the previous toppings in order before adding a new one. The only rule is that the topping--and the grosser the better--must be edible. With a small group, you should go around two or three times. Invite group members to help out those who have trouble remembering the toppings.

Note how frustrating it can be if you order something and don't get what you asked for—how frustrating it is, in general, when someone doesn't listen to you.

Desired Result:
To help youth identify poor listening habits and how it feels when someone doesn't listen to you.
(Choose Option A or B.)

2 chairs, small desk chalkboard and chalk or dry eraser board and marker
(Allow 10–15 minutes.)

CONNECT WITH THE SESSION

HEARING ISN'T LISTENING

A

Roleplay with another adult or older youth the following situation: You're seated in your office when a friend stops by to discuss a concern with you, such as a troubled relationship, a problem at work, school, or church, or just feeling stressed out. While the friend tries to talk to you, demonstrate habits of poor listening: distracted, not making eye contact, facing away, answering a phone call, interrupting, talking about yourself, and saying things that show you aren't listening. Your friend finally gives up on you and leaves. Overdramatize and keep the skit short (about three minutes).

ASK:

- **Could I hear what my friend said? Was I listening to my friend?**
- **What kinds of things did I do that showed you I wasn't listening?** (Write students' answers on a chalkboard or dry eraser board. Add poor listening habits they didn't name.)
- **How do you think my friend felt?**

B LISTEN UP, PARTNER

list of poor listening habits under the heading "Not Tuned In," chalkboard or dry eraser board, chalk or marker ***(Allow 10–15 minutes.)***

Tell youth that to be a good listener means you are tuned in to what someone is saying to you. Although you might not agree, you give your full attention and try to understand the other's point of view. One way to become a better listener is to learn what NOT to do when someone is talking to you.

Introduce the following items in the "Not Tuned In" column on the board: little eye contact, distractions (TV, loud music, noise, others around), doing something else, body turned away, interrupting, talking about self, easily distracted, not answering in ways that show understanding. Demonstrate each item. You may want to ask a youth volunteer to help you demonstrate.

Have youth pair off and sit facing each other. One partner is the poor listener, the other is the friend with the following problem: A teacher at school has accused the friend, along with some other students, of cheating on a test. The friend didn't cheat, but the teacher won't listen to any explanation. The friend's parents have been told, and they believe the teacher. To make things worse, the ones who really cheated want the friend to "take the fall" with them to show loyalty to their group.

Have the friends talk to the listener about their problem. While the friend talks, the listener acts out the poor listening habits listed on the board. After one to two minutes, have partners switch roles.

ASK:

- **How did you feel when you were talking and your friend didn't listen to you?**

CONNECT WITH THE BIBLE AND THE FAITH COMMUNITY

Desired Result:
Have youth consider that God always listens to them.

A GOD LISTENS TO ME?

Bibles, copies of the YouthPage, Youth Praise 3 (CD or tape, available from Cokesbury), CD or tape player ***(Allow 10 minutes.)***

Have youth turn to the Book of Psalms in their Bibles. Ask them to look through the Psalms for a minute, noting what they're about and the way in which they're written.

While youth do this, tell them the Book of Psalms is a collection of prayers and songs. Many were composed by people who wanted to tell God something. The people who wrote them knew they could talk to God about anything and that God would listen and always be with them.

Next, pass out pencils and copies of the YouthPage. Have youth read together Psalm 116:1-2.

Tell youth that the song they're going to hear, "Remember," is a modern-day psalm. It's printed on their copy of the YouthPage. While you play the song, have youth write their own psalm—or note to God—in the space provided on the student page. Remind them that they can tell God anything they want, whether it's a problem, a doubt, a regret, or a thank you—and God listens.

Have youth turn to the Book of Psalms in their Bibles. Ask them to look through the Psalms for a minute, noting what they're about and the way in which they're written.

While youth do this, tell them the Book of Psalms is a collection of prayers and songs. Many were composed by people who wanted to tell God something. The people who wrote them knew they could talk to God about anything and that God would listen and always be with them.

OR

If you have *Good News Bibles* or other Bibles youth find readable, have them read aloud together Psalm 116:1-2. Otherwise, ask a youth volunteer to read Psalm 116:1-2 as printed on the YouthPage.

Distribute paper and pencils, and have youth write a letter to God. They can tell God about a problem, a concern, or a worry. They can tell God about doubts they are having. They can express regrets about something they've done or thanks for something that God has done. Their letters will not be collected or read by others. Encourage honesty.

Remind the youth that the Bible tells us God always listens to us, but ask them to name other people in their church who care about them and who will listen to them. If youth aren't sure who to name, tell them there are Sunday school teachers, youth counselors, pastors, and other caring adults in their church whom they can talk to.

Desired Result:
Youth will practice active listening skills and consider how being a good listener helps them to be a better Christian.
(Choose Option A, B, or C.)

Stop, Look, and Listen poster
(Allow 10 minutes.)

CONNECT WITH LIFE

HEARING ISN'T LISTENING: PART 2

A

Remind youth that when God or someone else listens to us, we feel respected and cared for. When *we* are good listeners, we make others feel the same way. Being a Christian means caring for others and treating them with respect, which is what we do when we're good listeners. To be a good listener you should keep three things in mind: Stop, Look, and Listen. (Refer to poster.)

Briefly explain and demonstrate the "Stop, Look, and Listen" active listening skills described on the ReadMe page.

Reenact the "Hearing Isn't Listening" roleplay (see Connect With the Session). This time, however, tell youth to interrupt the roleplay whenever they see you being a poor listener. They should shout out the bad listening habits they see and correct you with active listening skills learned from Stop, Look, and Listen.

B LISTEN UP, PARTNER—AGAIN

(Allow 10 minutes.)

Remind youth that when God or someone else listens to us, we feel respected and cared for. When *we* are good listeners, we make others feel the same way. Being a Christian means caring for others and treating them with respect, which is what we do when we're good listeners. To be a good listener you should keep three things in mind: Stop, Look, and Listen. (Refer to poster.)

Briefly explain and demonstrate the "Stop, Look, and Listen" active listening skills described on the ReadMe teacher preparation page.

Have youth pair off as they did in "Listen Up, Partner" (see Connect With the Session), and remind them of the friend's problem from that activity. Have them take turns again being the listener and the friend (1 to 2 minutes each). This time, though, listeners should use the Stop, Look, and Listen active listening skills. Walk around the room during the roleplay. Answer any questions and help youth use a variety of the skills.

C HUDDLE UP

(Allow 10 minutes.)

Remind youth that when God or someone else listens to us, we feel respected and cared for. When we are good listeners, we make others feel the same way. Being a Christian means caring for others and treating them with respect, which is what we do when we're good listeners. To be a good listener you should keep three things in mind: Stop, Look, and Listen. (Refer to poster.)

Briefly explain and demonstrate the "Stop, Look, and Listen" active listening skills described on ReadMe.

Have youth break into small groups and move to different areas of the room. Appoint a volunteer in each group to act as coach for his or her team. Tell the groups you'll give them one minute to create a win/lose game situation for their team (they pick the sport). Then, give them a two-minute time out for a pep talk and strategy session with their coach. While huddled up, team members should use the Stop, Look, and Listen active listening skills while their coach is talking to them. As the "official," you walk around the room and check to see that the "players" are listening to the coach.

copy of closing prayer printed below
(Allow 1 minute.)

CLOSING CONNECTION

Have youth stand in a circle and bow their heads for prayer. Have youth repeat aloud after you Psalm 116:1–2.

PRAY:
"I love the Lord, because he hears me; *(youth repeat)*
he listens to my prayers. *(youth repeat)*
He listens to me every time I call to him." *(youth repeat)*
Help me, God, to listen to others. *(youth repeat)*
Amen. *(youth repeat)*

ReadMe

THIS IS WHAT YOU NEED TO KNOW ABOUT THE TOPIC.

WHY THIS UNIT FOR SUNDAY SCHOOL?

Collier's Dictionary defines *communicate* as "to make known or understood," to transfer information such as "facts, wishes, or emotions, from a source to a receiver." To love and care for others as God wants us to, we have to know what their needs are. Good communication skills help us listen to those needs and respond appropriately. They also help us treat ourselves and others with respect.

Sunday school is a great place for helping youth discover how styles of communicating relate to the Christian faith. A teenager who communicates poorly may feel lonely and may have unsatisfying relationships. Teenagers with good communication skills—who treat others with respect and understanding, assert their needs and feelings, and keep their emotions in check during times of conflict—will be better equipped for life's journey and for answering the call to Christian discipleship.

ADVANCE PREPARATION

Activities for this unit introduce youth to some basic communication skills. Study the skills described below. You will need to explain and demonstrate them during the sessions. Model them in class through your normal interactions with the youth.

Session 1: Listening Skills

Stop—what you're doing; get rid of distractions (TV, loud music, siblings, tapping fingers, etc.); give undivided attention.

Look—the speaker in the eyes; use body language to say, "I'm really listening." (Face speaker and lean in a close but comfortable distance; nod head occasionally.)

Listen—until you really understand speaker's point of view; keep quiet, especially about yourself; occasionally express understanding or empathy.

Session 2: Assertiveness Skills

How to send an assertive message:

- Describe the behavior causing the problem ("*When you* pressure me to smoke . . .")
- Say how it makes you feel ("*I feel* unhappy and stressed out . . .")
- Identify the effect of the behavior ("*because* it makes me feel bad and like you don't care about me.")

Session 3: Conflict Resolution Skills

Some guidelines for handling emotion-filled disagreements:

1. Treat the other person with respect.
2. Listen until you really understand the other's point of view.
3. Briefly and honestly state your own views, needs, and feelings without insulting the other person.
4. Keep your emotions in check, and let your reason determine what you say.

The communication skills outlined in this unit are adapted from *People Skills*, by Robert Bolton (Simon & Schuster, 1979).

TEACHER TIPS

Before class starts, have chairs arranged in a circle. Set up any audio/video equipment you need, check it out, and have it ready to go. Get all of your materials ready.

As youth enter the classroom, greet them individually. Learn their names and converse with them until it's time to start the lesson.

If youth will be using Bibles, have translations available that youth find easy to read and understand.

Be aware of the clock. Start and end on time. Keep the lesson focused and moving, budgeting your time as needed.

Affirm youth as they answer questions and participate in other ways during the sessions. Create an atmosphere where they feel comfortable asking questions and sharing their feelings and experiences.

KEY IDEAS IN THIS UNIT

For youth to make a connection between communication and faith, they must first understand that God always listens lovingly and acceptingly to them.

Communicating is such an integral part of relationships, but most people aren't very good at it. There are skills, however, that can help us get better. Teenagers can learn these skills and use them to enhance their relationships, get and maintain respect, and handle conflicts with others more productively.

TODAY'S YOUTH

With CDs, TV, computers, video games, and a host of school and extracurricular demands, a teenager's world is a world of distractions. When it's so easy to tune out, it makes it hard to really tune in—tune in to others and tune in to God.

Learning communication skills requires youth to try to see things from another's point of view and to respect it. This is especially challenging for younger adolescents who tend to be, developmentally, self-centered. Learning and using communication skills will help them focus on others. Also, by identifying the frustrations they have with communicating, younger youth can begin to understand the importance of being good communicators.

YOUTH PAGE

note to God:

A Psalm FOR Today

Remember
Words & music by Winston Baccus

I've been trying so hard
To be what I am inside
And sometimes it seems when I need you most
I forget you're by my side

And you know I wonder
What was I meant to do?
And sometimes I forget the promise
That I made to you
That I made to you
Oh, that I made to you

Sometimes my faith runs low
I feel I'm on sinking sand
But my foundation's on the rock
It's time to make a stand
It's time to make a stand
It's time to make a stand

Chorus:
Sometimes life can get real tough, and sometimes
it's not so much
And all I ever really need is the Master's loving
touch
We're building up the Body, we're reaching for
the sun
Gotta spread his love to everyone; the time has
gotta come

We travel down the lonely road, looking for our
way
But what we've all been looking for, I couldn't really
say

I'm searching north, and I'm searching south
Looking for the perfect love
And I'm searching east, and I'm searching west
But what I need comes from above.
What I need comes from above
What I need comes from above

Chorus

God help me to remember the price you paid for
me
God help me to remember all that I can be
All that I can be
All that I can be
All that I can be

from *Youth Praise 3* (CD/cassette available from
Cokesbury)

I love the Lord, because he hears me;
he listens to my prayers.
He listens to me every time I call to him.

Psalm 116:1–2 (*Good News Bible 2*)

SESSION 2:

I CAN'T GET NO . . . SATISFACTION (YES, YOU CAN)

Focus

To help youth develop assertiveness skills to communicate their needs and feelings in ways that respect others.

Scripture

1 Timothy 4:12

HERE'S THE PLAN | **DO IT YOUR WAY**

OPTIONS	TIME (minutes)	PREPARATION	SUPPLIES
INITIAL CONNECTION			
A Rhinoceros and Hippopotamus	5-7		an apple and banana, or two other items
CONNECT WITH THE SESSION			
A Space Invaders	10-15		chalkboard and chalk or dry eraser board and markers
B Satisfaction Survey	5-10	make copies of YouthPage	copies of YouthPage, pencils
CONNECT WITH THE BIBLE AND THE FAITH COMMUNITY			
A In Touch with Timothy	5-7	make copies of YouthPage, select music, bring tape/CD player	
B Sudden Impact	10	copy 1 Timothy 4:12 on posterboard	poster, notecards, pencil
CONNECT WITH LIFE			
A Assert Yourself	15	make copies of YouthPage	copies of YouthPage, note cards with case studies
B R-E-S-P-E-C-T (Find Out What It Means to Me)	10	make copies of YouthPage	Chalkboard and chalk or dry eraser board and marker
CLOSING CONNECTION			
Closing	3	Affirmation	

INITIAL CONNECTION

RHINOCEROS AND HIPPOPOTAMUS

With everyone seated in a circle, give an apple and a banana to one of the youth. Have the youth pass the apple to the person on his or her left, saying, "This is a rhinoceros." The person receiving it asks, "A what?" The passer answers, "A rhinoceros." The youth with the apple then passes it to the next person, saying, "This is a rhinoceros," to which that person asks, "A what?" The passer repeats the question to the first passer who answers, "A rhinoceros." The answer is passed down to the person with the apple. He or she then passes the apple to the next person, saying, "This is a rhinoceros." This progresses around the circle, with the question, "A what"? always going back to the first person with the apple. The answer, "A rhinoceros," is then passed all the way down to the youth with the apple.

Meanwhile, the banana is passed in the same manner to the right, but with the statement, "This is a hippopotamus." The rest of the routine is the same as the one for the apple/rhinoceros. At some point someone will get both items at the same time, and it gets even more confusing.

Desired Result:
To generate enthusiasm and get youth talking.

an apple and banana, or two other items
(Allow 5-7 minutes)

CONNECT WITH THE SESSION

SPACE INVADERS

A

Pair up youth with one of the persons sitting beside them. Have the pairs stand about a foot apart, facing each other. Next, ask them to move closer together until they're about three inches apart and introduce themselves.

After they sit back down, ask youth how it felt having someone stand so close to them. Tell them that if they felt uncomfortable it was because their "personal space" was being invaded. Your "personal space" can be your bedroom, your things, your locker, your body, and even your values, ideas, and opinions.

Write *Space Invaders* on the board, with these columns underneath:

My Turf	**My Stuff**	**Myself**

For about three minutes, have youth brainstorm items for each category. For example, "turf" could be bedroom, locker, desk, closet; "stuff" would be personal belongings; "myself" could be faith, beliefs. This last category may be difficult for them, so be ready to give examples.

Next, have youth identify space invaders for each column (no names, please). These may be siblings, parents, teachers, friends, pets. A space invader under "Myself" might be a parent who doesn't respect the youth's opinions or a friend who doesn't respect his or her values.

Desired Result:
Have youth consider how successful they are at standing up for themselves.
(Choose Option A or B.)

chalkboard and chalk or dry eraser board and markers
(Allow 10-15 minutes.)

copies of YouthPage, pencils
(Allow 5 - 10 minutes.)

ASK:

➤ **How do you feel when your space is invaded?**

➤ **How do you respond to space invaders? (Get angry? Don't respond? Ask invader to stop?)**

B SATISFACTION SURVEY

Distribute YouthPage and pencils. Have youth complete the Satisfaction Survey and the Rate How You Relate exercise.

ASK:

➤ **In what areas do you feel most satisfied? least satisfied?**

➤ **Who are some people who don't show you respect? In what ways?**

➤ **Does being a teenager have anything to do with whether or not you're treated with respect?**

Desired Result:
To have youth consider that they are the church of *today*, not just the church of the future. Youth should be treated with respect and also be good examples for others.
(Choose Option A or B.)

CONNECT WITH THE BIBLE AND THE FAITH COMMUNITY

copies of the YouthPage; "easy-listening" instrumental music on CD or tape; CD or tape player
(Allow 5 - 7 minutes.)

A IN TOUCH WITH TIMOTHY

Distribute YouthPage. Have youth volunteer to read the parts in the reading, "In Touch With Timothy." Start the music and let the reading begin. Youth without parts can read along silently.

ASK:

➤ **What did Timothy need to do, according to Paul, to be a good example to the church members?**

➤ **How could you make a greater impact on getting the church to change for the better, by being older or by being a good example? Why?**

SUDDEN IMPACT

B

note cards, pencils, poster with 1 Timothy 4:12 (copied from below)
(Allow 10 minutes.)

Have youth get in small groups of three or four. Give each group a note card and pencil and this assignment:

The pastor of our church has appointed your group to come up with suggestions for making our church better. Think about what our church could do to meet needs not being met or to make our church a better place for us to grow as Christians, worship God, or reach out to others. Whatever ideas you come up with, our pastor wants you to take a leadership role in making the changes.

After a few minutes have the groups make a brief report. Next, tell the class about Timothy, who lived during the early years of the Christian church. At that time a man named Paul was converting many people to Christianity. He also tried to encourage the young, local churches by visiting them and writing them letters. (Many of these letters are in the Bible.) Timothy traveled with Paul and helped him write some of his letters. Timothy was young, but he was a strong Christian. That's why Paul sent Timothy to help one of the churches that was having problems.

ASK:

- **How do you think Timothy felt about his assignment?**
- **How do you think he was treated by the older people in charge at the church?**
- **Do you feel that youth are respected in our church?**
- **Are there opportunities for youth to have input about what our church does?**
- **Should youth have that opportunity, or should they just wait until they're adults?**

Tell the class to read aloud together part of Paul's pep talk to Timothy: "Do not let anyone look down on you because you are young, but be an example for the believers in your speech, your conduct, your love, faith, and purity (1 Timothy 4:12, Good News Bible).

ASK:

- **What was more important to Paul than Timothy's age?**

Desired Result:
Have youth learn and practice assertiveness skills.
(Choose option A or B.)

copies of YouthPage, note cards with case studies
(Allow 15 minutes.)

CONNECT WITH LIFE

ASSERT YOURSELF

A

Tell youth that one helpful and appropriate way to stand up for themselves or to defend their space is to send an assertive message. An assertive message states the problem, how it makes them feel, and what effect it has on them. The message is sent in a way that isn't insulting.

— Have youth get in groups of three or four. Hand out copies of YouthPage. Give each group a note card with one of the following case studies:

— David never has any privacy in his room because his little brother constantly comes in and bothers him, but his mom doesn't want him to lock his door.

— Lindsay's friends have started smoking, but she hates smoking and doesn't want to do it. She's afraid of losing her friends, though, if she doesn't join them.

— Michael's girlfriend wants him to spend all of his free time with her. He doesn't want to lose his girlfriend, but he wants to do things with his friends, too.

— Jennifer wants to become a vegetarian. Her parents give her a hard time about it and ignore her requests at meal times.

Have youth review "Assert Yourself" on YouthPage. Tell the groups to write an assertive message for the teenager in their case study, using the "Assert Yourself" worksheet. After about five minutes, have groups share their assertive messages.

B R-E-S-P-E-C-T (Find Out What It Means to Me)

Chalkboard and chalk or dry eraser board and marker ***(Allow 10 minutes.)***

Tell youth that one helpful and appropriate way to stand up for themselves or to defend their space is to send an assertive message. An assertive message states the problem, how it makes them feel, and what effect it has on them. The message is sent in a way that isn't insulting.

Write on the board the column headings and accompanying phrases from "Assert Yourself" on YouthPage.

Ask youth to brainstorm things people do that really bother them, invade their space, or don't respect them. Have youth come up with an assertive message to send the "offenders" by completing the phrases under the headings on the board.

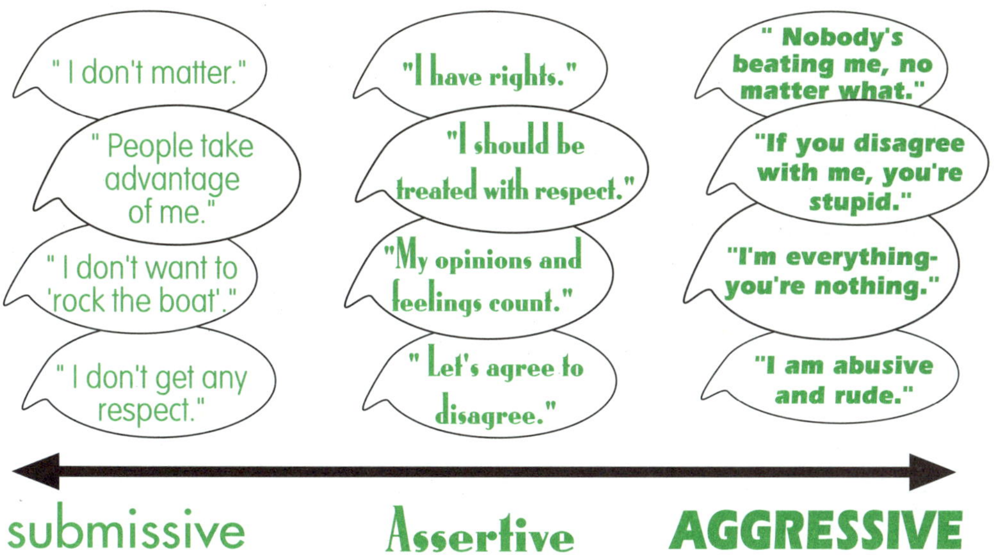

CLOSING CONNECTION

(Allow 3 minutes.)

Have the class stand in a circle, holding hands. Go around the circle, starting with the person on your left, and have each youth say, "I am only *(age)*." When it gets back to you, **SAY:**

➤ **As the Bible says, don't let anyone look down on you because you're young, but be an example in what you say, what you do, and how you treat others. You are the church of today. Go with God's blessing. Amen.**

I FEEL SATISFIED — YES, NO, MAYBE SO

Circle your satisfaction for each statement.

1. I can have privacy at home when I want it.	Y	N	M
2. Family members don't use my things without my OK.	Y	N	M
3. Friends don't "borrow" my things without my OK.	Y	N	M
4. My opinion is considered in major family decisions.	Y	N	M
5. My parents try to understand my side when we disagree.	Y	N	M
6. My needs and feelings matter in my family.	Y	N	M
7. My family/friends don't try to change my beliefs.	Y	N	M
8. My friends don't pressure me to go against my values.	Y	N	M
9. When I argue with someone, I usually "win."	Y	N	M
10. I tell others what I really want or how I really feel.	Y	N	M

IN TOUCH WITH TIMOTHY

(a reading based on Timothy 1)

Narrator 1: How would you feel if your minister told you about another church in town that was having problems, and then asked you to go help out? You'd have to tell the church's leaders that they were making some mistakes and that you were there to get them back on track. What would you do?

Narrator 2: This happened to Timothy in the early days of Christianity. Although he'd only been a Christian for a couple of years, his local church recommended him as a traveling companion to Paul, the famous missionary and church leader.

Paul: You come highly recommended, Tim. Your church tells me you're very committed to following Jesus Christ. You've learned a lot about our faith, and you try to practice its teachings. I need somebody like you to help me out on my missionary trips—maybe help me write a few letters to churches—that sort of thing. Are you interested?

Timothy: Sure. I'm up for it. I'd like to travel, see the sights, meet new people. I think I could learn a lot from you, Paul. I want to learn as much as I can about the Christian faith. There's a lot I don't understand and it would be an honor for me to go with you.

Narrator 1: Timothy became an important part of Paul's ministry. Paul trusted him and gave him more and more responsibilities.

Narrator 2: Paul thought of Timothy almost as a son instead of as just his partner. Then, one day...

Paul: Tim, I need you to do something for me.

Timothy: Anything, you name it.

Paul: Well, there's this church in Ephesus (EH-fuh-sus) that has a problem. Some men there are teaching things about our faith that aren't true, and their preaching needs to stop before the people start believing it and it harms the congregation.

Timothy: When do we leave?

Paul: No, Tim, I want you to go.

Timothy: Just me? Those men aren't going to pay any attention to me. What influence could someone my age have on the leaders and members of the church.

Paul: Tim, listen to me. Don't ever let anyone look down on you because you're young. It's your example that will make them respect you and take you seriously. Just be an example for the believers in what you say and do, and in your love, faith, and purity. Not only will you get their attention, you'll make a difference.

ASSERT YOURSELF - HOW TO SEND AN ASSERTIVE MESSAGE

Use these steps to fill in the chart below and send an assertive message.

1) Describe the behavior . Be specific; don't judge the behavior or insult the other person.
2) Describe how that behavior makes you feel. Be honest--don't exaggerate or downplay your feelings.
3) Describe the negative effect that the person's behavior has on your life.

WHAT YOU DO. . .	MAKES ME FEEL. . .	BECAUSE (EFFECT). . .
Example: When you borrow my stuff and keep it a long time...	I feel frustrated...	because then I don't have it when I want or need it

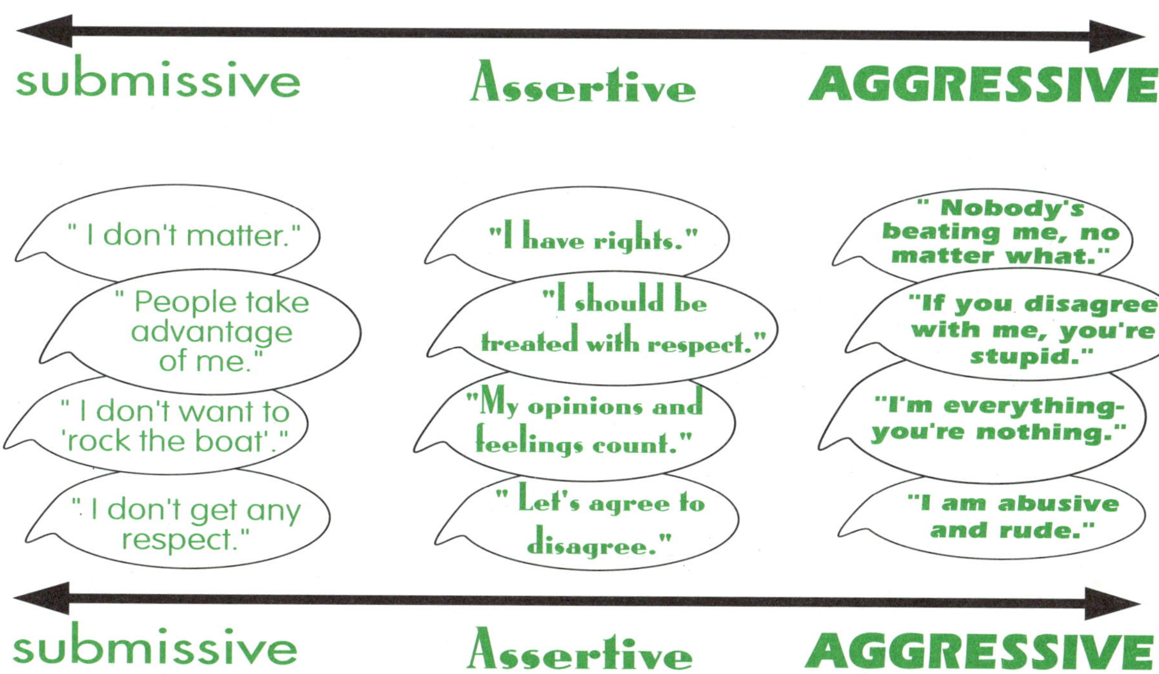

SESSION 3:
GETTIN' A GRIP ON IT

FOCUS

To help youth develop skills to deal with conflict in productive and appropriate ways.

SCRIPTURE

Ephesians 4:29, 31-32

HERE'S THE PLAN | **DO IT YOUR WAY**

OPTIONS	TIME (minutes)	PREPARATION	SUPPLIES
INITIAL CONNECTION			
Class Match-up	10	gather note cards	note cards, pencils
CONNECT WITH THE SESSION			
A The Young and Aggressive	10	videotape staged argument	prepared video, VCR, monitor or TV
B Bad News	10	gather newspapers	newspapers, red markers
CONNECT WITH THE BIBLE AND THE FAITH COMMUNITY			
A Conflict Cartoons	10-15		posterboard, pencils, markers, rulers, Bibles
B Conflict and Conduct	5		newsprint, markers
CONNECT WITH LIFE			
A The Young and Aggressive Revisited	10	make copies of YouthPage	YouthPage, VCR, video from Connect with the Session
B You Gotta Fight Right	15		YouthPage
CLOSING CONNECTION			
Pray	3		

INITIAL CONNECTION

CLASS MATCH-UP

Distribute note cards and pencils. Have each youth write on his or her note card an interesting but unknown fact about himself or herself. ("I've met the president"; I was born in China"; "I broke my leg when I was nine"; "I once painted my dog's nails.") The fact cannot identify them by gender ("My football team won the championship"), be visible to others, or be known by anyone else in the room. They are not allowed to show their cards to others. You'll probably need to give examples and repeat the rules to help them come up with their own facts. Tell them their cards will be read aloud to the class.

Collect the cards as they finish and mix them up. Read each card to the class and ask them to guess who it describes. Give the card to the person they guess. After all the cards and youth have been matched, have each youth say if he or she has the right card. Those holding cards with facts that do not match them must stand in front of the class and repeat the process. As a match is made, that person can sit down.

Desired Result:
Create a comfortable atmosphere and get youth talking.

note cards, pencils
(Allow 10 minutes.)

CONNECT WITH THE SESSION

THE YOUNG AND AGGRESSIVE

A

Tell youth they're going to see a dramatized argument between two teenaged friends. Tell them to notice, as they watch, what the argument is really about and the emotions that are involved.
Show the tape.

ASK:

➤ **What were the friends basically fighting about?**

➤ **What emotions were involved in this argument?**

➤ **Were they able to resolve anything, or work it out?**

➤ **What kinds of conflict do teenagers have in their lives?**

Desired Result:
Have youth identify conflict in their lives and the emotions that accompany it.
(Choose Option A or B.)

a 1 - 2 minute videotaped role play of two teenaged friends having a heated argument (insulting and accusing each other, but not violent); VCR and monitor
(Allow 10 minutes.)

copies of the newspaper, red or orange markers
(Allow 10 minutes.)

BAD NEWS

B

Have youth get in groups of four or five. Give each group a copy of the newspaper and a marker. Tell the groups to look through their papers and to circle and read any news story about a fight, argument, disagreement between people (two athletes fighting, two school board members arguing, two relatives having it out, etc.).

After a few minutes have the groups share their findings.

ASK:

- ➤ **What emotions were involved in these conflicts?**
- ➤ **Were the conflicts resolved, or worked out, in some way?**
- ➤ **Did emotions get in the way of resolving the conflicts?**
- ➤ **What kinds of conflict do teenagers have in their lives?**

Desired Result:
Introduce youth to biblical guidelines for dealing with conflict.
(Choose Option A or B.)

CONNECT WITH THE BIBLE AND THE FAITH COMMUNITY

sheets of posterboard, pencils, markers, rulers, Bibles
(Allow 10 - 15 minutes.)

CONFLICT CARTOONS

A

Have youth get in pairs or groups of three and make cartoon panels based on Ephesians 4:26, 29-32. The panels should illustrate the verses, with the corresponding verse or verse segment printed beneath each panel. Display the posters when the groups are finished. Invite them to share comments about designing their panels.

ASK:

- ➤ **According to these Bible verses, is it a sin to be angry?**
- ➤ **How can being angry make us sin or do something wrong?**
- ➤ **How does God want us to act when we're angry?**

CONFLICT AND CONDUCT

B

Ephesians 4:26, 29-32 written on newsprint, colored markers
(Allow 5 minutes.)

Tell youth that conflict has been around since Eve got Adam to bite the apple. Conflict is present in many of the Bible stories. Conflict is part of life. It's part of *our* lives. God is not going to remove conflict from our lives. God knows we're going to get angry at others. However, God expects us to handle conflict in certain ways.

Show youth the passage from Ephesians written on the newsprint. Tell youth the verses give us guidelines for dealing with conflict. Have youth turn the passage into a reading that the class can read responsively. Ask them to suggest different groups within the class to read specific verses or parts of verses. Give them some examples, such as girls, boys, people with blue eyes, 8th graders, etc. Use the markers to indicate the breaks in the verses and who reads what part. After readers are assigned for each part, have the class read aloud their responsive reading.

ASK:

➤ **According to these Bible verses, is it a sin to be angry?**

➤ **How can being angry make us sin or do something wrong?**

➤ **How does God want us to act when we're angry?**

CONNECT WITH LIFE

Desired Result:
Introduce youth to steps that will help them resolve conflicts in constructive, biblical ways.
(Choose Option A or B.)

THE YOUNG AND AGGRESSIVE REVISITED

A

copies of the YouthPage, the videotaped role play from "Connect With the Session"; VCR and monitor
(Allow 10 minutes.)

Hand out copies of YouthPage. Review the steps in "How to Fight Right." Ask youth if they can think of examples for each step. Tell youth you're going to show the videotaped argument they saw at the beginning of class. As they watch it this time, they should note how the Fight Right steps are not being used. After showing the tape, **ASK:**

➤ **What set the course for this argument — emotion or reason?**

➤ **What were the needs and view points of the two teenagers?**

➤ **How could the teenagers in this video have used the Fight Right steps?**

➤ **What Fight Right step would be most helpful for you?**

copies of YouthPage
(Allow 15 minutes.)

B YOU GOTTA FIGHT RIGHT

Have youth get in groups of two to four for role plays. Give each group a copy of YouthPage.

SAY:

➤ **Your role play assignment has two parts: First, decide on a conflict you want to act out. It could be a conflict that involved someone in your group, or you can make it up. It needs to be a conflict between a teenager and someone else like a friend, parent, sibling, or teacher. Each person in your group should help decide on the conflict and develop the role play, but not everyone needs to be in it. Secondly, the teenager in the role play must deal with the conflict using the steps in "How to Fight Right" on the Student Page and the verses from Ephesians we just read.**

Give the groups five minutes to plan the role play, then have each group do its role play for the class. After the roleplaying, **ASK:**

➤ **Why is it important to control your emotions when you're arguing with someone?**

➤ **What suggestions would you give someone on how to keep their cool?**

➤ **Are there certain times and places that are better than others for having an argument?**

➤ **What are ways you can treat the other person with respect, even if you're mad?**

(Allow 2 - 3 minutes.)

CLOSING CONNECTION

Invite youth to share concerns for themselves or others that they would like the class to pray about. Open the prayer and give youth an opportunity to pray aloud if they wish. As you close the prayer, pray for all the concerns not mentioned aloud by others. Pray for God's help to be understanding, forgiving, and loving during times of conflict.

HOW TO FIGHT RIGHT

1. Treat the other person with respect. Be courteous. No name calling.

2. Listen until you really understand the other's point of view. Say it out loud so the other person can tell you if you've got it right or not.

3. State your views, needs, and feelings briefly and honestly. Don't exaggerate or be dramatic. Choose your words carefully. Don't accuse or insult the other person.

4. Argue with your head, not your emotions. Try to reach an agreement based on understanding both sides and being reasonable. Be willing to compromise.

"THE BEST HUMAN RELATIONSHIPS USUALLY EXIST ON THE OTHER SIDE OF CONFLICT."

(*People Skills*, Bolton, page 231.)

BEING A CHRISTIAN— EVEN AT SCHOOL?

© CLEO PHOTOGRAPHY

SESSION 1: WHO AM I AT SCHOOL?

SESSON 2: TEACHERS AND TESTS AND RULES, OH MY!

SESSION 3: YOU CAN DO IT!

Purpose

This unit will explore ways to live out the Christian faith in everyday situations at school.

This Is Not Junk Mail!

IT'S IMPORTANT STUFF FROM YOUR TEENAGER'S SUNDAY MORNING LEADER

THEME TALK

For the next three weeks, your son or daughter will be learning about how to be a more faithful Christian at school. Youth best learn from their parents by example. If you openly live out your faith everyday, your adolescent will be more likely to follow in your footsteps.

FAITH FOCUS

Parents have always had a tough time in the comic strips. In *Calvin and Hobbes*, Calvin is constantly taking a poll to determine if he will be re-electing his dad to the office of dad for another year. Calvin is always complaining about what his mom cooks for dinner; often he imagines being chased by these casseroles on a strange planet. Calvin's best friend is his stuffed tiger, Hobbes. Hobbes comes to life when no one else is around, or so it seems to anyone else but Calvin. Hobbes is always alive and involved in the action from Calvin's viewpoint.

But Calvin leaves Hobbes at home when it is time to go to school. I guess he thinks that a tiger roaming the school halls might just shake things up a little too much, especially around lunch time. Some things just wouldn't look good on your permanent record.

I wonder how many youth leave Jesus behind at home or at church. If Jesus was really walking around school with your son or daughter, that just might shake things up. Some people feel nervous when Jesus is around, because they are reminded of their past. Other people are glad to see Jesus because He brings hope for their future and comfort, courage, and joy for today. Talk with your son or daughter about how they can be faithful to Christ at school and not leave Jesus at church.

SCHOOL STRESS

Teens face stresses at school today that are much more intense than those their parents had to deal with. In some areas, just going to school wearing the wrong color can be hazardous to your health. Youth deal with prejudice, guns, violence, AIDS, sexual temptations, suicide, cheating on tests, drugs, alcohol abuse, date abuse, and many other stressors. Most of these problems are not new, but the feelings of helplessness and hopelessness are burdens which our teens carry. They may wonder what life has to offer them. Even if they graduate from college, they are not guaranteed a good job, and most are aware that they will probably live below the economic level of their parents. It really is a jungle out there, but remember—Jesus is the king of the jungle!

THIS WEEK

Ask your son or daughter to really tell you about school life. Be careful not to interrupt or show your immediate disapproval, because this will cut the conversation short. Really listen. Let your adolescent know that you love him or her unconditionally. Tell him or her about what Jesus means to you and how you feel better when he is involved in your everyday life. Make a promise to each other to be strong Christians everywhere you go this week.

Hallelujah!

IDEAS FOR PEOPLE WHO PLAN WORSHIP

Key Scriptures
I Samuel 17:4–11,37–50.
Acts 3:2–12,16.
Acts 16:16–35.
Daniel 1:3–20.
1 Kings 19:9–13.

The purpose of these worship ideas is to provide resources to help make worship more youth friendly. **Share this with** your pastor(s), chair of worship area, musicians, and other people responsible for worship.

Popular Music

On any Sunday morning you will see, at best, most youth mumbling the words of hymns. At worst, they might be joking about the lyrics, writing notes, or just simply not paying attention at all. Encourage youth to rewrite some of the hymns to be more meaningful for them. Of course, if any youth take you up on the challenge, you will need to try to work their songs into worship. That is, after all, how Isaac Watts started writing songs.

Using original music and contemporary Christian music in worship sends the message to youth that they are valued, appreciated, and can contribute to worship

And The Band Played On

Contact your school band director and see if it might be possible to have the band play a couple of songs during a worship service. They will probably be able to find something appropriate. Even if it doesn't work out for them to play at worship, you will make the youth feel good by simply extending them the invitation.

C·R·I·S·I·S Counseling

Are there persons in your church who could help counsel youth during a natural disaster or personal crises? These types of contacts and training sessions need to be developed with school officials before an emergency actually occurs. In worship services, special speakers could be invited to church to reach out to the special needs of youth.

Let Youth Share

Invite some of the youth to talk about what it is like to be a Christian in their schools. How can the church support the youth in ways in which they might be strong Christians at school?

Miscellany

IDEAS FOR TEACHERS

If your class is a combined class of youth in grades 6–12, it may be helpful to know some of the differences you may encounter.

Younger Youth

Younger youth learn best by doing. They need active experiences. Try to get them involved by reading out loud, working in small groups, writing on the board, or other activities to engage their need to be active. Activities need to be brief, and they will not want to discuss a topic for a long period of time. They may need to be presented with a basic situation to talk about during a discussion, rather than inventing a relevant situation themselves. They might be embarrassed about talking about being a strong Christian at school if they have not had many role models from older youth. They may be more comfortable talking about an imaginary situation of taking Jesus with them to school, than a real life scene about being a strong Christian. They may be good at knowing what someone ought to do in a situation, but may not relate that well with their personal life and responses to real situations. They will be influenced by how they see older youth, youth leaders, and parents living out their faith.

Older Youth

Older youth can talk about their own responses to faith issues at school in more personal ways. They will be less likely to view situations as having a concrete right or wrong solution. They will be able to think of situations for discussion and might want to ask some tough and challenging questions about how their Christianity can make a difference in their school.

They will want to talk about gray areas in how they live for Christ at school, and they might not find a Christian witness as being relevant to their school life. They may separate church and home personalities from the way they act at school. They will more intensely feel the pressures to fit in and experience unhealthy activities.

Lydia Frogge

Read Me

THIS IS WHAT YOU NEED TO KNOW ABOUT THE TOPIC.

Church Life and Youth Culture

The Bible doesn't seem to make any distinction between sacred life and secular life, but youth today do. In the Bible there are not rules for how the average person should act at church, home, or school. Today, many youth seem to wear a different personality with their school friends than they do with their church friends. Their culture is not too friendly with Christianity. The culture does value seeking for truth and spirituality, but culture today is too tolerant to limit itself to finding all the answers in Christianity. Youth often end up with the idea that it doesn't matter what you believe as long as you believe in something that works for you.

Most youth live with the stress of trying to live up to society's, parental, or church leaders' expectations and demands. It is easy to admit that most youth are not prepared to deal effectively with the responsibilities of life, since suicide is the third leading cause of death among teenagers. There are many ways that youth can escape the responsibilities placed upon them and deaden the pain and guilt in life.

Most youth are afraid of being embarrassed by anything, anyone, and at anytime. They think that being a strong Christian might make them seem like a nerd or crazy. Youth often play down their feelings and beliefs to be accepted as part of a group.

You Don't Have To Surrender

With all the problems in the schools today, there seems like there is very little for our youth or our future. But you don't have to give up. Some youth are standing up for Jesus in visible ways in their schools. They don't have to wear a Christian T-shirt everyday or have a prayer meeting around the flag pole. These Christians are witnesses in their daily lives. Sure they fall sometimes, but their friends see their integrity when they admit and learn from their mistakes. These will be the witnesses that other youth seek out when they have a problem or crisis, because not only can they relate, but they have made it through a similar situation.

I Wish I Had All The Answers

Sometimes we, as teachers, wish we had all the answers. But that is just not realistic. We grow and mature through our experiences just as youth do. Teachers don't have to have all the answers, most youth probably wouldn't listen to you even if you did. All you need to do to be a good teacher is to be prepared (that is know your topic), enjoy being in relationships with the youth, and be open to God's lead.

Today's Youth

Generation X is a label that is being hung on today's youth. Most of them don't have goals in life, except perhaps to be rich and famous through sports, music, or being an entertainment celebrity. They don't have a single musical taste so alternative, rap, rock, pop, and country are all flourishing in the market. Youth gravitate to science fiction like The X-Files, but also like family comedies. All kinds of movies find youth audiences, but the everyday reality, mindless mayhem, crude, slapstick comedy, or dark conspiracy movies do especially well.

It seems that Generation X doesn't really stand for anything. You can just fill in the blank with anything and be right to some degree. In the Greek, the first letter of "Christ" is X (chi). Perhaps this Generation X could be a generation for Christ. Wouldn't that be amazing?

Church & State

The separation of church and state issues make many school administrators and boards very nervous. Elections are often won or lost because of these issues. Most schools would rather not have anything religious in them in order not to offend anyone. But this solution teaches morals without a foundation, and schools are reaping the harvest of this thirty-year-old policy. It is something like throwing the baby out with the bath water. The truth is that the founding fathers never expected for there to be a ban of religion in school. They simply did not want a state-sponsored official religion. If there are any clubs or groups that meet on campus, then a Bible club or Christian group may also meet on campus as long as it is run by the students (adults may also participate). That's the law.

In the Greek, the first letter of "Christ" is X (chi). Perhaps this Generation X could be a generation for Christ. Wouldn't that be amazing?

SESSION 1:

WHO AM I AT SCHOOL?

FOCUS:

To help youth be more comfortable with their faith when they are at school.

SCRIPTURE:

I Samuel 17:4–11, 37–50

HERE'S THE PLAN | **DO IT YOUR WAY**

OPTIONS	TIME (minutes)	PREPARATION	SUPPLIES
INITIAL CONNECTION			
Pop Quiz— Not Really	5–7		paper, pencils
CONNECT WITH THE SESSION			
A Allowed to Be a Christian?	10		
B The Toughest Thing for Me. . .	10		
CONNECT WITH THE BIBLE AND THE FAITH COMMUNITY			
A Sticks and Stones May Break My Bones. . .	10–12	provide Bibles for students	Bibles
B I Give You What I Have	10-12	provide Bibles for the students	Bibles
CONNECT WITH LIFE			
A Just People Like Us	5–8		
B Helping Others	5–8		
C Generally Speaking	5–10	copy the YouthPage prior to session	YouthPage
CLOSING CONNECTION			
Be Who You Are	10–12	copy the YouthPage prior to session	YouthPage

INITIAL CONNECTION

POP QUIZ—NOT REALLY

Ask the class members to each get a piece of paper and pencil. Tell them that there is going to be a quiz. Let them complain all they want; and when they are ready, ask the following questions to determine how much time they spend each week with school related activities.

ASK:

- **How much time do you spend each week traveling to and from school?**
- **How much time do you spend each week with extracurricular activities, games, and going back to school for activities?**
- **How much time do you spend each week studying?**
- **How much time do you spend each week actually being in school for classes?**

Then ask them to add up their weekly school time. Who spends the most time on school-related activities?

Desired Result:
To identify how much time is spent at school.

paper, pencils
(Allow 5–7 minutes.)

CONNECT WITH THE SESSION

ALLOWED TO BE A CHRISTIAN?

A

Ask the class to spend a couple of moments thinking about what is easy or difficult about being a Christian in their school. Then encourage them to discuss their thoughts. Use some of the following questions to spark the discussion.

ASK

- **When is it hard to be a faithful Christian at school?**
- **When is it easy?**
- **Can you wear Christian T-shirts and crosses or pass out flyers for Christian concerts and special programs at your school? Why or why not?**
- **Is there a bulletin board or some place that you can put up posters? Is there a free speech area?**

Desired Result:
To examine how difficult it may be to be known as a faithful Christian at school.
(Choose Option A or B.)

(Allow 10 minutes.)

(Allow 10 minutes.)

THE TOUGHEST THING FOR ME. . .

B

Ask the students to turn to a partner and to tell each other what the most difficult thing is for them, personally, about being a Christian at their school. Then discuss the issues as a class.

Desired Result:
To realize how some people in the Bible lived in God's will and were not limited by the logic of cultural wisdom.
(Choose Option A or B.)

CONNECT WITH THE BIBLE AND THE FAITH COMMUNITY

STICKS AND STONES MAY BREAK MY BONES. . .

A

Bibles
(Allow 10–12 minutes.)

S

Ask the class to make a list of what they would need to do if they had to go fight an enemy. What would they take with them to the battleground? Some youth may be pretty knowledgeable of some kinds of military hardware.

© Cleo Photography

Then ask the class if they might consider taking only a slingshot? What would the best military advisers' expert testimony be to that kind of strategy?

Ask the class if they know what battle was won by one guy, a slingshot, and a stone.

Let the class tell you the story of David and Goliath. If they do not know the story well, divide them into small groups and let them each read a part of the story to their group and be ready to tell their part to the whole class.

- I Samuel 17:1–11
- I Samuel 17:12–30
- I Samuel 17:31–40
- I Samuel 17:41–51

Let the small groups tell the story. Ask the class:

➤ **Wasn't it foolish to face a well-armed, experienced opponent like that?**

➤ **David was encouraged to wear Saul's armor. Why didn't he?**

➤ **David faced a giant by just being who he was and using the gifts and graces God had given him. How do you face situations that seem too big to overcome? With courage and faith like David's?**

➤ **David didn't try to be someone he was not. Do you think you could be a faithful Christian at school? After all, you don't have to face a giant that literally wants your head!**

B I GIVE YOU WHAT I HAVE

Bibles
(Allow 10–12 minutes.)

Let the youth get into small groups and look up one of the following passages.

- I Samuel 17:4–11, 37–50
- Acts 3:2–12,16
- Acts 16:16–35

Ask the groups to describe the situations and the people involved in the above Scriptures. What would be the common reaction of most people in that situation?

➤ **David should have been given armor that fit or not even been allowed to fight since he was not a trained soldier.**

➤ **Peter could have given the beggar some money, or taken an offering, or ignored him altogether.**

➤ **Paul could have run away when the earthquake opened up the jail doors. They all used the situation to point to God's power and glory by just being themselves and using the gifts and talents God had given them.**

Desired Result:
To identify ways the youth live out or hide their Christianity at school and how that affects their relationships.
(Choose Option A, B, or C.)

(Allow 5–8 minutes.)

S

CONNECT WITH LIFE

A JUST PEOPLE LIKE US

Ask the class to name any five people from the Bible. How do they think these people would fit into their school if they were the same age as the students and were new transfer students there tomorrow? Would they stand out? Would they go along with the crowd?

(Allow 5–8 minutes.)

B HELPING OTHERS

Ask everyone to turn to a partner and answer some questions. Give them time to answer each question before asking the next one.

- **When was the last time you helped a school friend with a problem? Were you influenced by your faith in the advice you gave?**
- **Is it easier to help a friend who is going through a difficult time if everyone knows that you are a Christian?**
- **Do friends seek you out to talk with because you are a Christian? Why or why not?**
- **In the Scripture you looked at, what difference did it make what faith the people had?**
- **Is it hard to just be yourself at school? Do you sometimes want to put on an act or a mask?**

GENERALLY SPEAKING

(Allow 5–10 minutes.)

Ask the group to make a quick list of the issues which are important to their friends and other students at school. Are there differences in opinion of what is right and wrong between your beliefs and those of the majority at school? Let the youth discuss their answers.

CLOSING CONNECTION

BE WHO YOU ARE

Desired Result:
To realize that being a Christian means being comfortable with your beliefs and values even at school.

(Allow 10–12 minutes.)
copies of the YouthPage for each youth

Pass out the YouthPages. Have a good reader read "The Stonecutter" from the YouthPage. Ask the class to explain how what happened to Thomas can connect with what we have been talking about. Discuss the questions in "The Bottom Line."

Encourage the students to be comfortable with their faith wherever they may be. With all the time spent at school, it would be tough to put on an act all the time. Encourage them to be themselves and not wish to be someone famous or more popular, because that just won't solve their problems in life.

Close with a time of prayer.

The Unhappy Stonecutter

There once was a stonecutter named Thomas. One miserably hot day he was cutting stone on the mountainside, as he did everyday, when the heat began making him weak. He looked up at the sun and thought that there was no more powerful force in all of nature. Thomas cried out, "God! Please make me the sun so that I will be happy." God answered his prayer and Thomas became the sun. So Thomas heated things up. He scorched the neighbors' fields and made everyone talk about how this was the hottest week they could ever remember. He was happy until some billowy clouds moved into town with a weather front ,and the people were relieved by the shade and stopped talking about the sun.

Thomas' anger burned within him. He did not like to be ignored. He thought that those clouds must be the most powerful force in all of nature if they could so easily block out the sun. So in his humility he cried out, "God, make me those clouds so that I will be happy." God answered his prayer and he became the clouds.

So Thomas blocked out the sun's light. The town began to miss the sun, and they feared that all of their crops would die without sunlight. Finally a big wind came through and blew the clouds away.

Well, Thomas could hardly contain himself with this development. As he was swept away he thought that this wind was definitely the most powerful force in nature. He cried out, "God, make me the wind so that I will be happy." God answered his prayer, and so Thomas became the wind. He blew trees and houses down and pushed people around. You might say he was happy, until one day, he blew up against a mountainside. No matter how hard he tried, he could not budge this big rock. He thought to himself, this mountain must be the most powerful force in all of nature, "God, make me this mountain so that I will be happy." God answered his prayer and he became the mountain. Through many years he stood. The sun, storms, and wind tried to knock him down, but he wouldn't budge. He was happy, until one day when a stonecutter came by and began to cut chunks out of the mountainside. Thomas cried out, "This little man is more powerful than I am; given enough time, there will be nothing left of me at all. What will I do?"

And God answered, "Thomas, why don't you just be who you are? Just be who you are!" And Thomas became a stonecutter again. He was finally happy to just be himself.

THE BOTTOM LINE

Do you know anyone like Thomas? The Bible tells a lot of stories about average people just being who they really were. They made a difference in the world because of their courage and faith. Does your faith make you happy? Does your Christianity make any difference in your relationships at school?

SESSION 2

TEACHERS AND TESTS AND RULES, OH MY!

FOCUS:

To help youth learn that having a positive attitude at school can help them enjoy what is already good and give them a better chance to try to change anything else.

SCRIPTURE:

Daniel 1:3–20.

HERE'S THE PLAN **DO IT YOUR WAY**

OPTIONS	TIME (minutes)	PREPARATION	SUPPLIES
INITIAL CONNECTION			
The Perfect School	10–12		
CONNECT WITH THE SESSION			
A The Good, the Bad, and the Ugly	10		
B My School—Caught on Tape	15	make and edit video prior to session	videotape, VCR, and TV
CONNECT WITH THE BIBLE AND THE FAITH COMMUNITY			
A Daniel's School	8–10	read the Scripture in advance	Bibles
B Dan Eats His Vegetables	10	read the Scripture and make copies of YouthPage,	Bibles, YouthPage
CONNECT WITH LIFE			
A If Daniel Were Here Today...	10–12		
B It's an Attitude Thing	10–12		
CLOSING CONNECTION			
Being Positive Is a Plus	8		

INITIAL CONNECTION

THE PERFECT SCHOOL

As they come in, divide youth into small groups or pairs and give them the assignment of creating the perfect school. Tell them that there must be learning times as well as fun and game times in their schools. Let the groups tell everyone about their perfect schools.

Desired Result:
To have fun creating the perfect school.

(Allow 10–12 minutes.)

ASK:

- **In what ways do you learn in the perfect school?**
- **What kind of fun, social, and recreation time do you have?**
- **Is there time to grow spiritually at your perfect school? Why or why not?**
- **On a scale of 1–10, how close is your perfect school to your real-life school?**

CONNECT WITH THE SESSION

Desired Result:
To examine the good and the bad things about school.
(Choose Option A or B.)

(Allow 10 minutes.)

A THE GOOD, THE BAD, AND THE UGLY

Let the youth tell you the best things about their schools. Then let them tell you the worst things about their schools. Then let them decide what the ugliest place in their school is.

B MY SCHOOL—CAUGHT ON TAPE

videotape, VCR, and TV
(Allow 15 minutes.)

This activity takes some advance planning. Get permission from the principal to videotape some places in the schools your students attend. Tape places like the lunch room, their lockers, classrooms, stairs, trees, and see if they can guess at which school or where these shots were taken. Then discuss the best and worst places in school.

Desired Result:
To realize that people in the Bible did not always have an easy time remaining faithful in their schools.
(Choose Option A or B.)

CONNECT WITH THE BIBLE AND THE FAITH COMMUNITY

A DANIEL'S SCHOOL

Bibles
(Allow 8–10 minutes.)

Let the class members each read a couple of verses of Daniel 1:3–20. (Some youth don't like to read out loud for varying reasons, so allow anyone who does not wish to read to pass.)

SAY:

➤ **What do think Daniel's school was like?**

➤ **They had to go to school, or what would have happened to them?**

➤ **Why do you think Daniel and his friends were blessed with health and knowledge?**

➤ **What would you have done in their place?**

B DAN EATS HIS VEGETABLES

YouthPage, Bible
(Allow 10 minutes.)

Have the class get into small groups or pairs. Tell the class the following situation, or let them read it in the YouthPage.

Dan and his three friends were in a boarding school away from home. The school administrators set the curriculum and the school lunch menus. Dan did not think the food was healthy, and asked if they could eat from a menu he came up with. Dan and his friends basically ate vegetables and drank water, instead of the rich food and alcoholic beverages the other students were eating and drinking. The four young men learned a great deal in school. They became especially knowledgeable about foreign languages, literature, and philosophy. Dan was known for his ability to find the answer to any puzzle or problem as well as being able to interpret dreams.

ASK:

- **Who do you think actually did better and remained healthier after three years in training? (Encourage them to support their answers with some reasons for this outcome.)**

After the small groups have had an opportunity to tell the class what they talked about, let everyone know that the situation is from the Bible, if they have not already figured that out.

Read Daniel 1:3–5, 8, 12, 15–20.

CONNECT WITH LIFE

Desired Result: To identify some ways youth can make their school experience better. **(Choose Option A or B.)**

A IF DANIEL WERE HERE TODAY. . .

(Allow 10–12 minutes.)

ASK:

- **How did Daniel and his friends make a difference in their school?**
- **What issues would Daniel take to heart to be faithful to God if he were in your school?**
- **Would you have tried to help the other students in Daniel's situation? How?**
- **What things would you like to see changed at school?**
- **What could you help change to make things better at your school?**
- **How could you start?**
- **How would you approach school authorities to talk about changes?**

B IT'S AN ATTITUDE THING

(Allow 10–12 minutes.)

Tell the class the following information and **DISCUSS** the questions:

- **Daniel and his friends had to go to school just like you do. They were forced to study some topics they probably didn't want to study. I'm sure there were a lot of things they would rather be doing.**

➤ What kind of an attitude did they seem to have? They gave it their best and they remained true to their faith.

➤ What kind of an attitude do you have toward school, teachers, and the rules?

➤ How can having a positive attitude help make it all work better?

➤ What are most important things you will learn from school?

Desired Result:
To encourage youth to have a positive attitude in life, even about school.

(Allow 10 minutes.)

CLOSING CONNECTION

BEING POSITIVE IS A PLUS

A

Read this to the class:

Someone once said, "You can catch more flies with honey than with Spam." Well I don't know if that is true or not, and I'm not really sure why anyone would want to catch a lot of flies anyway. Perhaps it is all about having a sweet, positive attitude toward life and relationships. In the novel, *Don Quixote* on which the musical *Man of LaMancha* is based, the main character did some strange things. The goofiest thing was to fight a windmill that he thought was an evil dragon. But he also seemed to see the potential in all the average people around him. The funny thing is that by the end of the story, they all have lived up to the potential he first saw in them.

I don't much care for Spam, but I do like honey on raisin bread. (I always check for flies.) Since you have to go to school anyway, you might as well find some good things while you are there. TREATING YOUR TEACHERS WITH RESPECT, LIKE YOU WOULD A GOOD FRIEND, WILL MAKE YOUR SCHOOL DAYS MUCH MORE ENJOYABLE. IF YOU LOOK FOR THE GOOD IN THEM, THEY WILL PROBABLY LOOK FOR THE GOOD IN YOU. Jesus also saw the great potential in people. Because of Jesus, some fishermen became miracle workers. An outcast woman he met at a well evangelized her town. A woman that no one would throw stones at got a second chance at life through forgiveness. A tax collector found honesty. Because of Jesus, I found forgiveness and new life also. Because of Jesus, you can find what you need to make your life a good thing.

Emphasize the positive attitudes about school, teachers, and studying that were discussed during the class. Ask for prayer concerns before you close with prayer.

TEACHER TIPS

Characteristics of Middle Schoolers

When teaching middle schoolers, always keep in mind that at these ages, growth and development will vary tremendously from one individual to another. The following characteristics are common of most middle schoolers.

Physical Development

- Grow in spurts.
- Have improved hand-eye coordination.
- Mature at different rates—girls earlier than boys.
- Have wide differences in individual physical development.
- Begin to mature sexually and have questions about emotional urges related to sexual development.

Interest in Knowledge

- Begin to challenge that what adults say is always true, and are no longer willing to accept whatever they are told.
- Can be reasoned with.
- Try to do things well and tend to be perfectionists.
- Are able to use reading to seek and share information.
- Have greatly increased attention spans and may spend several hours at an interesting activity.

Knowledge and Use of Bible

- Use the Bible in study and worship.
- Grow in their understanding of the relation between the Bible message and their own relationships with God.
- Explore the meaning of biblical passages by study and discussion.
- Learn how to use Bible references and table of contents.
- Become acquainted with sections of the Bible (the Law, the Gospels, and so forth).
- Can use different Bible translations and versions.
- Begin using reference books.

TEACHERS AND TESTS AND RULES, OH MY!

DAN EATS HIS VEGGIES

Dan and his three friends were in a boarding school away from home. The school administrators set the curriculum and the school lunch menus. Dan did not think the food was healthy, and asked if they could eat from a menu he came up with. Dan and his friends basically ate vegetables and drank water, instead of the rich food and alcoholic beverages the other students were eating and drinking. The four young men learned a great deal in school. They became especially knowledgeable about foreign languages, literature, and philosophy. Dan was known for his ability to find the answer to any puzzle or problem as well as being able to interpret dreams.

Who do you think actually did better in school and remained healthier after three years in training? Read Daniel 1:3–20 for the whole story.

Are you surprised that Daniel had to prove himself? His plan was tested for ten days to see if it might work. Have you ever had an idea for something good at your school that you could test?

TOP TEN LIST

Write your favorite things about school.

10.

9.

8.

7.

6.

5.

4.

3.

2.

1.

SESSION 3

YOU CAN DO IT!

FOCUS:

To help youth decide how to react faithfully to—and not always retreat from—difficult situations at school.

SCRIPTURE:

1 Kings 19:9–13

HERE'S THE PLAN | **DO IT YOUR WAY**

OPTIONS	TIME (minutes)	PREPARATION	SUPPLIES
INITIAL CONNECTION			
Rock, Scissors, Paper	5–8	learn the game	
CONNECT WITH THE SESSION			
A Pop Quiz	8–10	make copies of YouthPage	YouthPage
B Name That Stress	10–15	make one or two lists of school stresses & secure supplies	large sheets of paper, non-permanent markers or crayons
CONNECT WITH THE BIBLE AND THE FAITH COMMUNITY			
A You Don't Always Retreat—Sometimes You've Got to Advance	10	read the Scripture and think about what it could mean to different people in a variety of situations, make copies of YouthPage	YouthPage
CONNECT WITH LIFE			
A Be Strong	8–10		
B Wish They Knew	10–12	secure materials before class time	large sheet of paper, marker, and tape
CLOSING CONNECTION			
X Marks The Heart	12–15	secure materials before class time	large sheet of paper, marker, tape

Desired Result:
To break the ice and introduce the pressure to succeed.

(Allow 5–8 minutes.)

INITIAL CONNECTION

ROCK, SCISSORS, PAPER

Let the class members find a partner and play the hand game (rock crushes scissors, scissors cuts paper, and paper covers rock). The winners should then continue to play each other until there is only one champion. The winner doesn't get anything but the satisfaction of being good (and lucky) at the game.

ASK:

- **Did anyone really want to win this game?**
- **Did anyone try to cheat?**
- **How does the winner feel about being the champion?**
- **Did anyone not want to play? Why?**
- **Does everybody else feel like losers?**

Desired Result:
To identify the stressors and pressures that youth experience at school. **(Choose Option A or B.)**

YouthPage
(Allow 8–10 minutes.)

CONNECT WITH THE SESSION

POP QUIZ

A

Ask the youth to work with a partner to answer the questions in the "Pop Quiz" section of the YouthPage. Then allow youth to tell the class what they talked about with their partners.

B NAME THAT STRESS

Large sheets of paper, non–permanent markers, or crayons
(Allow 10–15 minutes.)

Divide the class into two or three teams. Each team sends someone to you to begin the game. Show them the top word on your list of school stresses.

Sample list of school stresses from which to choose:

teachers	pop quizzes	beer parties
mid–terms	drugs	report cards
algebra	ugly gym uniforms	gangs
failing a test	guns	term papers
book reports	sexual temptation	cheating on tests
your permanent record	the principal's office	detention
a note to your parents		

Then send them back to their team to try to draw the stress until someone guesses the word or phrase. Then the next person runs up for a word. The game is over when all the teams have guessed all the words. Remind those who are drawing that they can't speak, grunt, make noises of any kind, or write letters or numbers on the paper.

Let the class tell you about the worst stresses at school. **ASK** them:

➤ **How do you resist these things?**

➤ **Why can't everyone always resist doing things that are harmful to them?**

CONNECT WITH THE BIBLE AND THE FAITH COMMUNITY

A YOU DON'T ALWAYS RETREAT—SOMETIMES YOU'VE GOT TO ADVANCE

Desired Result:
To help youth realize that we don't always have to wait for a retreat or a flashy program to hear God's will for our lives.

YouthPage
(Allow 10 minutes.)

Ask the class to read 1 Kings 19:9–13 silently to themselves, and to think about what it means for them.

Give the class some time to discuss the meaning of this passage. Help the youth realize that we don't always have to wait for a retreat or a flashy program or speaker to hear God's will for our lives.

SAY:

➤ Elijah has some major stress in his life because the authorities want to kill him. So he runs away and hides and gets depressed. God asks Elijah what he is doing hiding in a cave in retreat. He has just won a big victory for God over the prophets of Baal. God's voice within Elijah's heart is saying, "What are you doing here in retreat? You need to be in my service. It is not always easy to be faithful in what sometimes seems to be a faithless society. Return and do what I tell you to do."

CONNECT WITH LIFE

Desired Result: To explore ways to be a strong Christian at school. **(Choose Option A or B.)**

A BE STRONG

(Allow 8–10 minutes.)

Ask the students to think about some times at school, with school friends, or at school activities, when they wish they had shown a stronger witness. Have them turn to a partner and talk about ways they could have a strong faith at school.

Let the group discuss the issues about being a strong Christian at school. Some youth will be outspoken about their faith at school, and some might almost be embarrassed to let others know that they are a Christian.

Ask the group to think of some ways they can be faithful Christians and still be sensitive to other people's feelings and needs. Make up a couple of situations to test their ideas.

B I WISH THEY KNEW

Large sheet of paper, marker, and tape
(Allow 10–12 minutes.)

Ask the youth to turn to a partner and make a quick list of five things they wished their friends and everyone at school knew about Christians and faith in Jesus.

Let the partners tell the whole group what their choices were. Someone should record these on a large sheet of paper. (Avoid writing the same basic ideas.) **ASK** the group why they would like everyone to know these things. How would all this help you to be a stronger Christian at school?

Desired Result:
To encourage youth to stand for Christ through all the pressures.

Large sheet of paper, marker, tape
(Allow 12–15 minutes.)

CLOSING CONNECTION

X MARKS THE HEART

A

Draw a big X on the board or a large piece of paper. Ask the class to list all the things that this symbol could mean or stand for.

Write the word "generation" in front of the X and ask what this means to them now.

Tell the class that in Greek you would pronounce X as chi. Chi is also the first letter of Christ.

ASK:

➤ **Can all of you agree that you want be a generation of Christ and not a faceless, purposeless, fill-in-the-X group that doesn't stand for anything?**

SAY:

➤ **Sometimes Jesus calms the storm. Sometimes Jesus comforts us through the storm. Isn't it always better to be with Jesus, even in the storms of life, than to be alone?"**

ASK:

➤ **Are there persons you'd like to request prayer for; do you have concerns you'd like to discuss or have us pray about? Can we offer praise for things that are going well?**

Close with a circle prayer. Encourage students to let Jesus help them weather the tough times at school or anywhere.

TEACHER TIPS

Characteristics of Middle Schoolers

Last week's "Teacher Tips" looked at the physical development, interest in knowledge, and knowledge and use of the Bible. This week "Teacher Tips" concludes by looking at three other areas of middle school development.

The following characteristics are common of most middle schoolers.

Awareness of Self and Sense of Life Work

- Become increasingly independent.
- Tend to accept the values of their peer groups.
- Want to make their own decisions.
- Are building in their own minds an image of who they are as individuals.
- Become fairly responsible and dependable.
- Want to be useful.
- Desire to do something about wrongs in the world.
- Speak of what they would like to be when they become adults.
- Develop the ability to evaluate the way others have invested their lives.

Relationships With Others

- Experiment with acceptable ways of relating to other persons—with peers of both sexes, youths, and adults (parents, teachers, and so on).
- Feel intensely about unfairness, injustice, and social evils; have a strong sense of right and wrong.
- Are interested in and informed about people around the world.

Relationships With God and Sense of the Meaning of Life

- Ask deeper questions about God.
- Relate religious ideals to decision making.
- Begin to understand historical relationships and their significance.
- Begin to determine their own moral behavior in terms of understanding God's will.
- Express religious thoughts in words.
- Begin to identify with the religious community and its work.
- Explore the meaning of commitment to God through Jesus Christ.
- Grow in their understanding of the meaning of membership in the church.

YOU CAN DO IT!

POP QUIZ

Name the five worst pressures you deal with at school.
How do you resist these things?
Why can't everyone always resist doing things that are harmful to them?

1.
2.
3.
4.
5.

RETREAT or ADVANCE?

Read the Scripture below and write down what it means to you.

At that place he came to a cave, and spent the night there.

Then the word of the Lord came to him saying, "What are you doing here, Elijah?" He answered, "I have been very zealous for the Lord, the God of hosts; for the Israelites have forsaken your covenant, thrown down your altars, and killed our prophets with the sword. I alone am left, and they are seeking my life, to take it away." He said, "Go out and stand on the mountain before the Lord, for the Lord is about to pass by." Now there was a great wind, so strong that it was splitting mountains and breaking rocks in pieces before the Lord, but the Lord was not in the wind; and after the wind an earthquake, but the Lord was not in earthquake; and after the earthquake a fire, but the Lord was not in the fire; and after the fire a sound of sheer silence. When Elijah heard it, he wrapped his face in his mantle and went out and stood at the entrance of the cave. Then there came a voice to him that said, "What are you doing Elijah?" (1 Kings 19:9–13)

Let's face it—it isn't always easy to be a good little Christian at school. When you mess up, the other students might kid you with a snide line like, "I thought you were supposed to be a Christian?" Does being a strong and faithful Christian at school mean always being perfect? What do you think? What does the phrase "Generation X" mean to you?

CARING FOR CREATION

© CLEO PHOTOGRAPHY

SESSION 1: THE CREATION STORY: WHAT'S IN IT FOR ME?

SESSION 2: OUR ENDANGERED PLANET

SESSION 3: STEWARDS OF THE EARTH

Purpose:

This unit will help youth examine the biblical background related to the Creation Stories, and then help them discover why and how it is part of their Christian responsibility to take care of our earth.

This Is Not Junk Mail!

IT'S IMPORTANT STUFF FROM YOUR TEENAGER'S SUNDAY MORNING LEADER

FAMILY ACTIVITY

Think about some simple activities your family could do to help save the earth. Perhaps you could plant flowers around your house or commit yourselves to taking a monthly walk and picking up trash in your neighborhood. How could your family conserve more energy or water? Could each family member plan to take shorter showers? Could you keep your house cooler in the winter? Perhaps you could use cloth towels instead of paper towels. Talk about these ideas and others that your family might think of.

A CHARGE TO CARE

A CHARGE TO CARE I HAVE,
A GOD TO GLORIFY,
CARE FOR THE WORLD AND ALL OF LIFE
ON EARTH AND IN THE SKY.

A STEWARD OF THE EARTH,
PLANTS, WATER, CREATURES, TREES.
MY GOAL IN LIFE, MY JOY AND LOVE:
MY LORD AND GOD TO PLEASE.

I HEAR GOD'S CHARGE AGAIN,
"SEE THAT MY EARTH IS KEPT."
YES, LORD, I PLEDGE MY LIFE TO YOU,
YOUR TRUST, I NOW ACCEPT.
AMEN

ABOVE & BEYOND RECYCLING

Make a list of the things that your family already recycles. What else could you recycle that you are not currently recycling? Think about how you might recycle more than just newspaper, glass, aluminum and tin. Could you add regular paper to your list? How about cardboard boxes? Have you ever considered clothing to be a recyclable item? Do you give your unwanted clothes to charity or to other families that might make use of them? You might also recycle clothing by selling it at a consignment store in your area. How about organizing a family yard sale to recycle other household items? Our landfills are filled with small appliances, plastic kitchenware, and toys that other people could make use of, but which many people just throw away in the trash each day. We are a society that idolizes disposable things. Think about trying to organize a neighborhood yard sale involving everyone!

Hallelujah!

IDEAS FOR PEOPLE WHO PLAN WORSHIP

SCRIPTURE RELATED TO THIS UNIT
Genesis 1:-2:3
Genesis 2:4-3:20
Genesis 6:9-17
Psalm 65
Matthew 19:16-30

Music Suggestions:
"For the Beauty of the Earth"
"America the Beautiful"
"All Creatures of Our God and King"

QUESTIONS TO ASK ABOUT OUR WORSHIP

How much paper do your bulletins use? Have someone interview your church secretary and find out how much paper is used on a weekly basis to print your church bulletins. How much does your church newsletter take?

If you have more than one worship service, encourage your parishioners to recycle their bulletins. Ask to meet with your pastor or worship committee and suggest that one Sunday your church have a service (around Earth Day, April 22) in which bulletins are not used at all. Before the service begins, write out on a large chalkboard the hymn, liturgy, and Scripture page numbers. Or if your church has an overhead projector, write down all the page numbers and the litanies and prayers on a sheet to show on a screen.

LITANY

Psalm 8, adapted

O God, our God, how majestic is your name in all the earth!
Your glory above the heavens is chanted by the mouths of babes and infants.
You have founded a bulwark because of your foes,
To still the enemy and the avenger.
When I look at the heavens, the work of your fingers, the moon and the stars which you have established;
What is humanity that you are aware of us, and our children that you care for them?
Yet you have made us little less than yourself, and crowned us with glory and honor.
You have given humanity dominion over the works of your hands;
You have put all things under our feet,
All sheep and oxen, and also the beasts of the field,
The birds of the air, and the fish of the sea, whatever passes along the paths of the sea.
O God, our God, how majestic is your name in all the earth!

From *Bread for the Journey*, edited by Ruth C. Duck (The Pilgrim Press, New York, 1981); page 77.

Miscellany

IDEAS FOR TEACHERS

GRADES 6 TO 12

If you have all the youth of the church in one class, you might want to try some of the following suggestions to expand the unit for the older teens.

PROJECT LEADERS

Hopefully during this three-session unit your class will decide to embark upon some type of project to live out their faith as Christian stewards of the earth. Once your class has chosen a project, try to see that your older teens are given more responsibility in carrying it out. If you break into small groups, assign them as the group leaders. They could also be more willing and capable if you need to interview your pastor or other church committee heads before you launch your project.

SLIDE SHOW OR VIDEO TAPE

If it appears that you are losing your older class members, give them a special assignment to keep them interested in the topic. If your church owns a video camera or if you can borrow a 35mm camera, set them loose on a fun project. Ask them to design a video tape or slide show which contrasts the beauty of nature with the destruction that humans bring to it. Depending upon where you live, they might be able to take pictures of scenic sights in your immediate area (or it could just be shots of trees and flowers) and then contrast that with pollution (anything from trash on the ground to a nearby polluted stream or factory belching smoke). They could plan this project one Sunday, work on it during the week (they will probably need a parent's help) and then show it to the class at one of the two following sessions. They could also use taped music or narration in the background.

PLAN A WORSHIP SERVICE

The older youth in your class could plan a worship service around the theme of being good stewards of our earth. This service could be offered as a special worship time on Earth Day at the end of April, or you could arrange with your pastor to have the youth lead it during a Sunday morning or Sunday evening worship time. With your pastor's permission, they could write or find songs, liturgy, prayers, and Scripture related to the topic of "Stewardship of the Earth." If they do the above activity making slides or a video tape, that could also be included in the service. The youth would need to meet with your pastor after they have planned the service. Ask your pastor if he or she would be willing to work a sermon up that reinforces the theme.

SESSION 1:

THE CREATION STORY: WHAT'S IN IT FOR ME?

FOCUS

The creation stories have a lot to tell us about our responsibility as stewards of the earth.

SCRIPTURE

Genesis 1:1-15

HERE'S THE PLAN | **DO IT YOUR WAY**

OPTIONS	TIME (minutes)	PREPARATION	SUPPLIES
INITIAL CONNECTION			
A Creative Creature	10		newspaper, paper plates, cups, egg cartons, margarine tubs, foil, toilet paper tubes, plastic bottles, packing material, boxes, strong glue.
B Collect Trash	10		trash bags, gloves
CONNECT WITH THE SESSION			
A Creation Accounts	10		Bibles, newsprint
B Newspaper Wall	5		markers, newspapers, masking tape
CONNECT WITH THE BIBLE AND FAITH COMMUNITY			
A Guided Imagery	10		
B Write a Poem	15	make copies of YouthPage	YouthPage for each student
C Pretend You Are God	10	make copies of YouthPage	YouthPage for each student
CONNECT WITH LIFE			
A Noah's Ark Revisited	5		Bibles
B Write a Covenant	10	photocopy covenant or make one	newsprint, markers
C Create Your Own Eco-System	10		several two-liter soda bottles with lids, bag of soil, funnel, seeds (grass or flower), water
CLOSING CONNECTION			
Sing Together	3		

Desired Result:
To get the class ready for the upcoming unit.
(Choose Option A or B.)

INITIAL CONNECTION

A CREATIVE CREATURE

newspaper, paper plates, cups, egg cartons, margarine tubs, foil, toilet paper tubes, plastic bottles, packing material, boxes, strong glue.
(Allow 10 minutes)

SAY:

➤ **Use the items of trash and glue to construct some type of creature. You have only ten minutes to do this so work quickly.**

Place the finished creatures in a central location in the room where they can be displayed during the unit.

B COLLECT TRASH

several large trash bags, inexpensive surgical gloves
(Allow 10 minutes.)

S

SAY:

➤ **We're going to spend the first ten minutes of our class today picking up trash around the church.**

AFTERWARD ASK:

➤ **Were you surprised at how much or how little you found?**

CONNECT WITH THE SESSION

A CREATION ACCOUNTS

Desired Result:
To look at the first creation story and examine what significance it has for us.
(Choose Option A or B.)

Bibles
(Allow 10 minutes.)

S

SAY:

➤ **Before we read over the Creation story as it is told in the first chapter of Genesis, let's try to reconstruct it from memory.**

On a chalkboard or newsprint, challenge the class to try and remember what God created on each of the seven days.

NEXT:

Pass out Bibles and turn to Genesis 1:1-2:4. Choose two people to read as Narrator and as God and have them read the Creation account.

Then reread Genesis 1:28.

ASK:

➤ **What do you think it means to have dominion over something? Do you think subdue means to conquer and control?**

B NEWSPAPER WALL

markers, newspapers, masking tape
(Allow 5 minutes.)

S

SAY:

➤ **The universe that God created for us has many awesome as well as awe-inspiring aspects.**

➤ **On the newspaper write with large letters one thing from nature that God has created that you think is either awesome (thunderstorms) or awe-inspiring (sunsets). Write as many as you can think of and tape them to the wall or a chalkboard.**

After everyone has taped their newspaper to the walls, take a moment to read through all the ideas aloud. (Point out that newspaper was used so as not to waste paper.)

ASK:

➤ What does the Bible tell us about everything God created? (It was good.)

➤ Does this confuse you? Is it hard to acknowledge that everything God created is good? What are some of the things that God created that you would question as being good? (such as tornadoes)

➤ Is there any part of nature that you would question God about if you could?

Desired Result:
To examine what it means for us to be in charge of creation.
(Choose Option A, B, or C.)

CONNECT WITH THE BIBLE AND FAITH COMMUNITY

GUIDED IMAGERY

A

(Allow 10 minutes.)

S

➤ Turn off the lights in the room; tell the class to get comfortable and close their eyes. Then read the following paragraph very slowly and with a great deal of drama.

You are taking a hike in a very densely populated forest. The sky is a beautiful shade of blue with some white puffy clouds that you can just barely see through the trees. The sunshine pours in through the forest. The day is warm but not hot. It is Spring and the flowers and plants are just beginning to come into bloom. You take a deep breath and smell the wonderful piney smell of the trees all around you. You begin to walk slowly, and beneath your feet is the spongy feel of soft moss mixed with beds of pine needles. You hear birds singing, insects buzzing, and the breeze whispering through the trees as you walk. Soon you hear another sound, the sound of water rushing. You continue walking toward the sound, and around the next bend you come upon a beautiful waterfall. The spray from the small waterfall is creating a rainbow in the sun. Slowly open your eyes.

ASK:

➤ Can you recall a time when you felt at one with nature?

➤ What is the time of year you feel happiest to be outside?

➤ Adam and Eve felt very much at home in their beautiful garden. What parts of our world seem especially beautiful to you?

➤ Do you think the beauty of our world is threatened?

B — WRITE A POEM

YouthPage for each student
(Allow 15 minutes.)

S

SAY:

➤ **One way we can become more aware of nature around us is to write a poem called a cinquain. Look at your YouthPage to see an example of how it is written and the format to follow.**

Tell everyone to try to write a cinquain. Ask them to choose a theme from nature (trees, plants, animals, storms, sunsets, etc).

When they are done, choose a few to read and then display all of the cinquains around the room. Encourage everyone to read these after class.

C — PRETEND YOU ARE GOD

YouthPage for each student
(Allow 10 minutes.)

S

SAY:

➤ **Pretend you are God watching your children destroy what you have created. Write a letter to your children telling them how you feel about what they are doing to your earth and begging them to be better stewards of the gift you have entrusted to them.**

➤ **Use the space on the YouthPage for your letter.**

CONNECT WITH LIFE

Desired Result:
To begin to think of ways that we as individuals can make a difference in helping one another to be good stewards of the environment.
(Choose Option A, B, or C.)

A — NOAH'S ARK REVISITED

Bibles
(Allow 5 minutes.)

S

SAY:

➤ **Earlier we looked at the creation story in Genesis 1. For a few moments, let's read Genesis 6:9-17** (Noah's Ark).

➤ **Basically the story is about how God was displeased with the faithlessness of humankind. He sent a flood to destroy the earth. Noah's faithfulness pleased the Lord, so God commanded Noah to build an ark and fill it with two of every kind of living thing. God saved Noah, Noah's family, and the animals. After the flood waters receded, he set a rainbow in the sky as a sign that he would never again destroy the earth by flood.**

➤ **God has promised never again to destroy the earth by flood. But what about those of us who inhabit the earth today? Do you think we are destroying the earth ourselves?**

covenant photocopy
(Allow 10 minutes.)

S

B WRITE A COVENANT

SAY:

➤ **In the Noah's Ark account we read about how God made a covenant with us to never again destroy the world by flood. We have been entrusted as the caretakers of the earth. We have been given a great gift. Do we have a responsibility to save the earth from destruction?**

➤ **As a class we're going to write a covenant today. We'll begin by saying, "We (fill in the name of your class and church) agree to be caretakers of the earth that has been entrusted to us by God."**

➤ **Then we'll list the things we promise to do. After the covenant is finished I want everyone to come up and put their signature at the bottom of the paper. (Use covenant on page 79 or create one.)**

several two-liter soda bottles with lids, bag of soil, funnel, seeds (grass or flower), water
(Allow 10 minutes.)

C CREATE YOUR OWN ECO-SYSTEM

Give each person or each small group an empty two-liter soda bottle. Use the funnel to have them put a few inches of soil in the bottom of the bottle. Give them some seeds to sprinkle in too, and some small sticks. After they have watered the soil, they can put the lid back on and place the bottle in a sunny place in the classroom or in the church.

SAY:

➤ **God has created just the perfect balance of air, soil, and water on the earth. God created it all and then set his children on it to enjoy it and to take care of it. It is part of our job as God's stewards to help keep nature in harmony.**

CLOSING CONNECTION

CELEBRATE NATURE

SAY:

➤ **What are some ways we can celebrate nature? (hug a tree?) What can you do to show God that you appreciate the world that's been created for us?**

Even if your class doesn't like to sing, encourage everyone to join in singing "America the Beautiful" or some other appropriate song.

Covenant for Keeping the Earth

"We ______________________________

agree to be caretakers of the earth
that has been entrusted
to us by God."

We promise to:

____________________ ____________________

____________________ ____________________

____________________ ____________________

____________________ ____________________

____________________ ____________________

____________________ ____________________

Signed ______________________________

____

____

Date ____________________

Read Me

THIS IS WHAT YOU NEED TO KNOW ABOUT THE TOPIC.

POINTS TO CONSIDER

This unit should be of interest to your students. Most likely they have discussed it in-depth at school, although you will be putting a somewhat different spin on the topic since you'll be coming at it from a Christian perspective. Part of this unit involves looking at what the two accounts of the Creation story in Genesis have to teach us about our responsibility toward the earth. During the reading and discussion of the Genesis accounts of the Creation, it is quite likely that one of your students will question the stories as being just that, "stories." Remind your class that when they study the environment in school, they are doing so from a scientific perspective. They are looking at how human beings interact with the natural world. During this unit you are taking a personal and biblical look at your relationship with the planet on which you live. Try not to let the class get too hung up on the Creation stories, since this unit is merely using the study of the stories to help them better understand what God requires of us in regards to tending to the environment.

A LOOK AT THE 2 CREATION ACCOUNTS

The two accounts of the Creation in the Bible are indeed somewhat different. Scholars believe that they were written by different authors and that the first account, Genesis 1:1-2:3, was written several hundred years earlier than Genesis 2:4-25. The first account emphasizes humanity's place in the cosmos, whereas the second account takes place strictly in the Garden of Eden. Many scholars tend to look at the Genesis accounts as interpretive explanations of God's presence and our relation to the world.

TREAT it Well

There is an old African proverb which says:

Treat the earth well. It was given to you by your parents. It was loaned to you by your children.

Throughout the session you will want to stress to your class that we have been entrusted with a precious gift and we have a responsibility to take care of the earth so future generations can also enjoy it.

USEFUL RESOURCES:

To Heal the Earth, by Frederick Quinn, Upper Room Books, 1994.

The Next Step: 50 More Things You Can Do to Save the Earth, by the Earth Works Group. © 1990. Andrews and McMeel. A Universal Press Syndicate Company. Kansas City.

Caring for God's World: Creative Ecology Ideas for Your Church, Kristen Kemper, ed., Educational Ministries, Inc., Prescott, AZ, © 1991.

Two Minutes a Day for a Greener Planet, by Marjorie Lamb. © 1991. HarperCollins West, Scranton, PA.

YOUTHPAGE

THE CREATION story

Line 1 Two syllables
Line 2 Four syllables
Line 3 Six syllables
Line 4 Eight syllables
Line 5 Two syllables

Example:
Flowers
Beautiful blooms
Glorious gifts from earth
God's personal paintbrush in Spring
Growing

My Cinquain:

____
____
____
____
____

Dear Children,

Shalom,
Your God and Creator

SESSION 2:

OUR ENDANGERED PLANET

FOCUS

To emphasize each person's stewardship responsibility.

SCRIPTURE

Matthew 19:16-30

HERE'S THE PLAN | DO IT YOUR WAY

OPTIONS	TIME (minutes)	PREPARATION	SUPPLIES
INITIAL CONNECTION			
A Polluted Pennies	5	secure supplies ahead of time	vinegar, salt, small bowls, water, paper towels, many dirty pennies
B Aluminum Can Contest	5	collect soda cans ahead of time	several bags of washed out aluminum soda cans.
CONNECT WITH THE SESSION			
A House Fire	7		paper, pencils
B Ecological Quiz	5	make copies of YouthPage	YouthPage, pencils
CONNECT WITH THE BIBLE AND THE FAITH COMMUNITY			
A Take a Stand	5	tape line on floor	classroom or hallway floor, masking tape
B What Does the Bible Say?	5		Bibles
C Changes You Could Make	15		newsprint, markers
CONNECT WITH LIFE			
A Does Your Church Do Its Part?	10		chalkboard or newsprint, marker
B Recycle Ideas	5		paper, pencils
C Create a Commercial	20		paper, pencils
CLOSING CONNECTION			
Prayer			

Desired Result:
To engage the class in a fun activity before you begin today's session. **(Choose Option A or B.)**

INITIAL CONNECTION

A — POLLUTED PENNIES

vinegar, salt, several small bowls, water, paper towels, many dirty pennies ***(Allow 5 minutes.)***

SAY:

➤ **I've got all these dirty pennies and I want you to help me wash them.**

Instruct class members to wash them in the bowls of water.

After all the pennies have been dunked, ask the class if the pennies look any cleaner. (They won't.)

Suggest they try soap on them along with the water. (They'll still be dirty.)

Next pull out the bottle of vinegar you've had hidden. Empty the water bowls and pour 1/2 cup of vinegar into them as well as five tablespoons of salt. Then ask youth to bathe the pennies in this mixture. (They should come out very shiny.)

SAY:

➤ **This experiment can help us to see what pollution is like. We can ignore the problem and just keep trying to deny it doesn't exist, or we can try different solutions until we clean up our world.**

B — ALUMINUM CAN CONTEST

several bags full of washed out aluminum soda cans. If your class is large you'll need a lot! ***(Allow 5 minutes.)***

Break the class into several small groups and give each class a bag of aluminum cans. Tell them that when you say "go," they are to try and build the tallest structure they can in three minutes. Try it again giving them only one minute to build it.

CONNECT WITH THE SESSION

A HOUSE FIRE

Desired Result:
To begin examining ecological issues.
(Choose Option A or B.)

S

SAY:

- **You arrive home one day to find your house is on fire. The fire chief tells you that you have time to run back into the house and pull out five things. What five things would you choose?**

- **List them on the paper.**

- **In pairs compare your answers.**

NEXT SAY:

- **Our answers probably indicate that we are very materialistic. Did anyone think of family members or pets?**

Read the following poem to the class:

LETTING GO

It makes sense!
If I can afford it,
If I can make payments,
I'll buy it for myself.
I earned it!
I deserve it!
It's for me!

But I need God's help
  to sort out my real needs,
  to discipline my wants,
and to share what God has given me
  with others.

by Dorsey H. Walker, from *Alive Now*, March/April 1983, © 1983 by The Upper Room; page 20. Used by permission.

B ECOLOGICAL QUIZ

YouthPage, pencils
(Allow 5 minutes.)

S

Have everyone take the quiz on the YouthPage to see how familiar they are with ecological terms.

Afterward, go over the answers on the bottom of page 90.

Desired Result:
To examine our lifestyles.
(Choose Option A, B, or C.)

CONNECT WITH THE BIBLE AND FAITH COMMUNITY

A TAKE A STAND

(Allow 5 minutes.)

S

Before class begins, take a piece of masking tape and tape a line down on the floor of the classroom. Make sure it is placed in an area so that students can stand on it. If your room is too small, move the tape to the hallway.

SAY:

➤ **Think of this line taped to the floor as a continuum with the right end being "I totally agree" and the other end being "I totally disagree."**

Explain to them that the points in between these two extremes are represented by the rest of the tape.

Then read them the following statements and have them take a stand by standing on the tape to indicate their level of agreement.

Statements:
1. America has the wealthiest population in the world, and we should share that wealth.
2. It is a sin to be wealthy.
3. Wealthy people will not go to heaven.
4. We are a very wasteful society.
5. Christians should not have a lot of money.
6. If our families do have money, we should give it all away to the poor and live in poverty ourselves.
7. America uses more natural resources than any other country in the world.

B WHAT DOES THE BIBLE SAY?

Bibles
(Allow 5 minutes.)

S

SAY:

➤ **Let's read over Matthew 19:16-30.**

ASK:

➤ **Does this passage make you uncomfortable? Why or why not?**

➤ **As Americans are you aware of the fact that we have the most extravagant lifestyle in the world? And that we also are the most consumption oriented society on the earth?**

➤ **Did you know that less than 5% of the world lives in the United States; yet, as a country, we consume more than 16% of the world's energy production?**

C CHANGES YOU COULD MAKE

newsprint, markers
(Allow 15 minutes.)

S

On a large sheet of paper list these headings and leave space underneath to write lists:

Food Energy Lifestyle

Ask group members to suggest specific actions that they could take in each of these areas to lead a more responsible life as a Christian steward of the earth. (See Teacher Tips for some ideas.)

CONNECT WITH LIFE

Desired Result:
To examine things we might do to help the environment and become better stewards.
(Choose Option A, B, or C.)

A DOES YOUR CHURCH DO ITS PART?

chalkboard or newsprint, marker
(Allow 10 minutes.)

S

SAY:

➤ **In the past ten years it has become quite common for individual families to recycle in their homes. Many communities across the United States now have curbside recycling which makes it quite simple to recycle. But think about our church; are we doing our part?**

➤ **Let's make a list of ways we could be recycling here, and then try to determine if we could be the instruments to make that particular recycling effort possible. (See Teacher Tips for suggestions.)**

B RECYCLE IDEAS

paper, pencils

S

➤ **We are the wealthiest nation in the world; we are also a "throw-away society." We throw things away with very little thought as to whether they might be used again.**

➤ **What is the definition of the word recycle? (Use it again!)**

On a large sheet of paper, first have everyone list one item they have thrown away in the last week.

Next, on a large sheet of paper, quickly brainstorm a list of as many recyclable items as you can think of.

ASK:

➤ **Are there things you throw away that you could recycle?**

➤ **How would you rate your own families on recycling?**

paper, pencils
(Allow 20 minutes.)

S

CREATE A COMMERCIAL

Break your class into groups and ask each group to come up with a skit, or "commercial," encouraging more people to recycle.

Leave time for the class to perform some of the skits.

Video tape them if your church has a camera.

CLOSING CONNECTION

As a class, read over the prayer which they will find on their YouthPage.

After you have read it through together, try reading it in different ways. Go around the room and give everyone a phrase. Or read it loudly and then read it softly.

Read Me

THIS IS WHAT YOU NEED TO KNOW ABOUT THE TOPIC.

TEACHER TIPS

OUR ENDANGERED PLANET

LESSONS TO LEARN

One of the best ways to begin solving the pollution problem is to start by learning to respect and care for our earth. We are living in a world in which natural resources are bring depleted at an alarmingly fast rate. All Christians are called to be good stewards of the earth's resources. But what kind of lifestyle truly reflects being a good ecological steward? This session will begin to look at the many dimensions of good stewardship and suggest possible obtainable lifestyle changes that we should all consider to make our world a better place in which to live.

MAKING THEM SQUIRM

If your church is made up of fairly affluent people, the questions about Americans and their wealth might make some of your students uncomfortable. You may need to point out that wealth is not bad, it just means that you have more opportunities to try and make a difference by helping others. Also, try to make them understand that our entire society is consumer oriented, which is not healthy. As Christians we must remember that we are in the world but not of the world.

CHANGES YOU COULD MAKE

Remind your group that Americans are the most affluent society in the world. We are also a wasteful society. We use more of the earth's resources than any other nation. Perhaps it would be more accurate to say that we don't use them, we waste them. Our throw-away mentality and our consumer-oriented society do not make us model stewards, but there are simple lifestyle changes we could all work on, which would not make us any less comfortable but which would help save the earth.

Here are some ideas to help your class get started:

— Turn off lights when you leave a room.

— Keep your showers short.

— Make sure the dishwasher and washing machines are full before you run them.

— Do not let the water run continually when brushing your teeth.

— Car pool with others whenever possible; or ride a bike or walk!

— Encourage your family to turn down your thermostat a few degrees in the winter and up a few degrees in the summer.

— Don't open and close the refrigerator door more than you have to.

— Have your family add extra insulation around doors and windows.

— Try not to use so many paper cups and paper towels.

DOES YOUR CHURCH DO ITS PART?

Under Option A of Connect with Life, your class is to brainstorm ways in which your church could do more to contribute to the recycling effort. If your class has trouble getting started with this, offer them the following suggestions and see if they can then add to the list.

- If you have a coffee hour on Sunday mornings, are paper cups used? Styrofoam®?
- When you have potluck suppers does everyone use paper plates and plastic utensils?
- Do you have recycling bins set up around your church for paper, glass, and aluminum cans?
- When you have picnics or festivals outdoors where soft drinks are served, do you make sure you have recycling bins set out?
- Does your church office collect their used paper in a recycling box?
- Are church members recycling bulletins? If you have more than one service, they can do this by placing them in a box on their way out the door.
- If your church has a soda machine, is there a recycling bin set up next to the machine? Is it emptied regularly?
- If your church has church-wide catered dinners, are all the recyclable items from the kitchen taken to a recycling center by someone?
- Does your church have curbside recycling like many homes do in communities across the United States? If not, could you find out how to get it?
- Does your church ever sponsor a rummage sale so that church members can recycle their unwanted clothing and household items?
- Does your Sunday school waste paper? Could you order recycled paper?
- What is done with your old Sunday school curriculum? Could it be donated to another church in your area after you have used it?

GLOBAL WARMING

Global warming is not discussed at any point in this unit, but it may come up as a question from a student, since it is a "hot" topic right now. Global warming is a problem because of the recent increase of carbon dioxide and other gases in our air, caused mostly by industry and vehicles . These gases are contributing to a gradual warming of the earth. Although it is happening very slowly, it is quite a problem as it causes the sea level to rise and threaten coastal regions. Global warming can also affect growing seasons; and, if it continues to rise indefinitely, it could become too warm for many inhabitants on the earth.

YOUTHPAGE ECOLOGICAL QUIZ

Answers: 1. (4)

2. (3)

3. (6)

4. (1)

5. (2)

6. (8)

7. (5)

8. (7)

Ecological Quiz

Try and match up the words on the left with the definitions on the right:

List A	List B
1. biosphere	1. the act of bringing the world into ordered existence
2. pollution	2. capable of being broken down by microorganisms
3. ecosystem	3. environmental deterioration of air, water, food, and soil that may become a direct or indirect threat to life
4. creation	4. the part of the world in which life can exist
5. biodegradable	5. the preservation of rivers, forests, soil, and other natural resources
6. environment	6. the web of intricate biological relationships among plants, animals and microorganisms
7. conservation	7. to reuse materials one or more times after initial use
8. recycle	8. natural surroundings, conditions, influences

PRAYER FOR PRESERVING THE EARTH

God of the universe, you placed the earth in our trust; help us preserve it wisely, to understand dominion as responsible partnership with you, and not senseless exploitation of the world's resources. Save us from greed. Give us the gift of prudent lifestyles; of treasuring the simple gifts of earth; and of air, light, and water.

Help us to cherish the earth in all its mystery, treasure its fragile beauty, and honor its diversity; help us to turn from the paths of selfishness and destruction; let all creation reflect God's wonder and all creatures, in their own voices, sing God's praise. Amen.

Items on this page from *To Heal the Earth*, by Frederick Quinn (Upper Room Books, © 1994); pages 127 and 145.

SESSION 3

STEWARDS OF THE EARTH

FOCUS

To become more aware of what is happening to our earth's resources and to devise ways we might become better stewards.

SCRIPTURE

Genesis 2:4-3:20
Matthew 6:25-34

HERE'S THE PLAN | DO IT YOUR WAY

OPTIONS	TIME (minutes)	PREPARATION	SUPPLIES
INITIAL CONNECTION			
A Make a Rain Storm	5		
B Read *The Lorex*	10	need *The Lorex* book	*The Lorex* by Dr. Suess
CONNECT WITH THE SESSION			
A What Do You Know?	5	make copies of YouthPage	
B How Many Resources Do You Use in a Day?	15		paper, pencils
CONNECT WITH THE BIBLE AND FAITH COMMUNITY			
A The Other Creation Story	10		Bibles
B Jesus' Use of Nature	15		Bibles
C Helping Our Faith Community	15		newsprint, markers
CONNECT WITH LIFE			
A Sponsor a Poster Contest	10		
B Challenge Yourself	5		paper, pencils
C Challenge Your Church	10		chalkboard
CLOSING CONNECTION			
Closing	5		balloon, marker, pin

INITIAL CONNECTION

A MAKE A RAIN STORM

Desired Result:
To get the class focused on the unit topic.
(Choose Option A or B.)

(Allow 5 minutes.)

S

SAY:

➤ **As a class, we're going to create a thunderstorm. The person on my right will do everything that I do. The person next to them will do the same action, and we will continue around the room adding each person until we're all doing the same action. Then I will move onto the next action.**

-Misting: Rub palms of hands back and forth
-Sprinkling: Snap fingers
-Hard Rain: Slap your thighs with your palms
-Thunderstorm: Stamp feet

When all have joined in the thunderstorm, reverse the movements and do it backwards, having each class member drop out of each movement until everyone has stopped and the rainstorm is over!

© ROBERT CAMPBELL

B READ *THE LOREX*

The book by Dr. Seuss called The Lorex, (Random House, 1971). You can probably find this at your public library.
(Allow 10 minutes.)

Read this book to the class and get their reaction to it.

Desired Result:
To get the class to think more about what they know about the earth's environment and how they use the earth's resources daily.
(Choose Option A or B.)

CONNECT WITH THE SESSION

A WHAT DO YOU KNOW?

YouthPage, pencil
(Allow 5 minutes.)

S

SAY:

➤ **Look at the YouthPage and take the True/False quiz there to get a feel for how well informed you are.**

When everyone is finished, go through the correct answers given at the bottom of Teacher Tips for Session 3.

Afterward ask the class if they were surprised by any of these statistics.

B HOW MANY RESOURCES DO YOU USE IN A DAY?

paper, pencils
(Allow 15 minutes.)

S

SAY:

➤ **We tend to take for granted how many natural resources we use each day.**

➤ **Write down a general outline of what your day looks like, starting with the time you wake up.**

➤ **For each step of your day write down what natural resources you use. (Examples: alarm clock wakes you up—electricity; take a shower—water heated by natural gas; ride bus—gasoline)**

When everyone is done, **SAY:**

➤ **You have been looking at how you, one teenager, use up the world's resources everyday; but multiply your use by all the people there are around the world depleting our earth's resources everyday.**

NEXT ASK:

➤ **What resources are being depleted in our country and in the world?**

➤ **Are we developing replacements for any of these resources?**

➤ **Do you think we can take natural resources for granted?**

CONNECT WITH THE BIBLE AND FAITH COMMUNITY

Desired Result:
To look at what the Creation story teaches us about being stewards, as well as a look at some other biblical references.
(Choose Option A, B, or C.)

A THE OTHER CREATION STORY

Bibles
(Allow 10 minutes.)

S

ASK:

➤ **In Session 1 of this unit we looked at the Creation story in Genesis 1, but did you know there is another account of the Creation in the Bible?**

Have them turn to Genesis 2:4-3:20. During this reading, ask for several volunteers to pantomime the different parts as the story is read by the narrator. Select volunteers to be Adam, Eve, the serpent, and God.

After the passage has been read, ask the class which part of the second Creation story they think has the real message for us as God's children.

Suggest they reread Genesis 2:15. This line tells us what we are to do with the earth. We are to "till it and keep it."

ASK:

➤ **What do you think that line means?**

NEXT:

Read to the class the explanation as to why there are two different Creation accounts in Genesis. (See Session 1 Read Me.)

B JESUS' USE OF NATURE

Bibles
*(**Allow** **15 minutes.**)*

S

SAY:

➤ **Jesus also used many images taken from nature in his teachings. (He used yeast, wheat, vines, mustard seeds, trees.)**

Ask everyone to spend a few minutes looking through the Gospels and locating one of Jesus' nature teachings. (Matthew 13 has several to choose from.)

Suggest that they think of a way to pantomime that for the class. Choose a few students to do theirs and guess what passage it is.

Finish by reading Matthew 6:25-34.

Chalkboard or large sheet of paper, marker, ***(Allow 15 minutes.)***

S

HELPING OUR FAITH COMMUNITY

C

ASK:

➤ **Why do you think it's critical for Christians to take the lead in environmental issues?**

As a class, brainstorm a list of all the things we can do to help save our earth. Make this list as exhaustive as possible.

Contact your church newsletter editor after class and ask if this list can be put in the next newsletter. If your church doesn't have a newsletter, perhaps the list can be printed as an insert for your bulletin one Sunday, around Earth Day, April 22.

Desired Result:
To help the class begin to look at things they can do to make a difference.
(Choose Option A, B, or C.)

CONNECT WITH LIFE

SPONSOR A POSTER CONTEST

A

paper, pencils ***(Allow 10 minutes.)***

S

SAY:

➤ **One thing we might do as a class to begin to get our church family to think more about recycling and saving the environment would be to sponsor a Poster Contest called "What Can I Do to Clean up the World?" for the children of the church. After the posters are completed we could hang them up around the church for several weeks or have them on display in the fellowship hall.**

As a class decide when the contest will start, what ages it will be for, what the prizes will be, and who will judge the posters. Elect a student to draw a flyer about the contest and have someone hand it out in the children's Sunday school classes.

small slips of paper, pencils, basket ***(Allow 5 minutes.)***

S

CHALLENGE YOURSELF

B

Hand out to everyone a slip of paper and have them write down on it one thing they plan to do personally to help save our environment. Tell them to write it like this: I commit myself to help my family start a compost pile. Or, I commit myself to buying only food that is packaged in recyclable packaging.

After everyone is done, have them put their slip in a basket. Then pick up the slips and read through them. (No one should sign their name to them.) Afterward offer up a simple prayer, asking God to help your students to carry out these commitments.

CHALLENGE YOUR CHURCH

chalkboard, newsprint, markers
(Allow 10 minutes.)

SAY:

➤ **Although we are only one small cog in the whole environmental picture, we can make a difference. Let's think of a plan of action that we could share with our church to encourage us to begin to become better stewards. We can educate the entire congregation.**

Have the class brainstorm ideas and then choose one to implement. Discuss how you will carry it out. Choose a delegation to represent your class at your church's official board, or administrative body meeting, or arrange to present the plan to your pastor. (For further ideas, see Teacher Tips.)

CLOSING CONNECTION

large green helium balloon, marker, pin
(Allow 5 minutes.)

Before class, buy a large green helium balloon. With a marker draw simple representations of the continents on it. Also have a pin ready so that you can pop it.

For closing have the class read Psalm 19 together.

Then get the helium balloon. Tell class members this is to represent the earth. Have everyone stand up and begin batting the balloon around the room.

Remind class members that God has created us to be the caretakers of the earth, and that as God's stewards we have a responsibility to help save the world from destruction.

After the balloon has gone around the room several times, tell someone to bat it back to you. Then before they know what has happened, pop the balloon with the pin.

SAY:

➤ **If we don't care for the earth, who will? We have been entrusted with a very fragile gift and if we are careless, it will never survive for future generations.**

Hold hands and encourage each student to offer up one thing they will do to help save our earth. After each statement say: "Lord, we are your caretakers; help us we pray." End with a group "Amen."

Read Me

THIS IS WHAT YOU NEED TO KNOW ABOUT THE TOPIC.

TEACHER TIPS

STEWARDS OF THE EARTH LOOKING AHEAD

Hopefully from the first two sessions your class has gotten the message that indeed the future of our planet is in danger. We are using up the earth's resources faster than they can be replenished. We are running out of space to put the mountains of garbage we generate each year. In many parts of our country and the world, we are continuing to pollute the air and water. This session will help your class begin to formulate tangible ways they can help make a difference in cleaning up God's world.

HELPING OUR FAITH COMMUNITY

One of the questions you will be asking your youth in this session is why it is important for Christians to take the lead in environmental issues. Point out to them that we can make a difference. We have a direct role in caring for the universe which God has entrusted to us. We are a faithful people and faith leads to action. Throughout history Christian churches have often been the forerunners in taking the lead on important issues.

CHALLENGE YOUR CHURCH

Hopefully your class will come up with a plan of action to present to the entire congregation. This should be an action plan to get your entire church family more involved in recycling, eliminating pollution, or further cleaning up the environment. Your class can take the lead in this endeavor!

Here are a few ideas your class might want to explore:

- Recycle more at the church and at church functions.
- Educate the congregation about how to begin and maintain a home compost pile to help cut down on yard wastes.
- Adopt a polluted river in your county and pledge to clean it up.
- Find out if nuclear waste is a problem in your area. If it is, start a letter-writing campaign to your local elected officials.
- If your church doesn't have a yearly rummage sale, suggest that one be started to help parishioners recycle unwanted household items, and at the same time raise money for the church!
- Start a car pooling plan to link people who live near each other that could ride together to church meetings and events.

WHAT DO YOU KNOW?

ANSWERS TO QUIZ ON YOUTHPAGE

Take the True and False Quiz below to see how well informed you are regarding environmental issues.

1. Experts say at the current consumption rates, the world's known oil reserves will be used up in 80 years. (T OR F) **False (35 years)**

2. Burning fossil fuels is the main cause of the greenhouse effect or global warming. (T or F) **True**

3. The world population has more than doubled since 1950. (T or F) **True**

4. By the time an American reaches 75, he or she will have produced 5 tons of garbage, used 6 million gallons of water, and used two times as much energy as the world average. (T or F) **False (52 tons of garbage, 10 million gallons of water, 5 times as much energy)**

5. Each of us is responsible for contributing to the greenhouse effect. (T or F) **True**

6. Americans use an average of 100,000 aluminum cans every week. (T or F) **False (1.5 billion)**

7. About 30 acres of the earth's forests are destroyed every minute. (T or F) **False (80 acres)**

8. Every ton of recycled paper Americans buy saves 17 trees. (T or F) **True**

9. It takes 500 recycled milk jugs to make a six-foot plastic park bench. (T or F) **False (1,050 milk jugs)**

10. Americans drive the distance to the planet Pluto and back every day. (T or F) **True**

11. Each year, do-it-yourself oil changers improperly dump more oil than the tanker Exxon Valdez spilled into Alaska's Prince William Sound. (T or F) **True**

12. Every year Americans discard 1.1 million tons of disposable plates and cups. This is enough to set a picnic for everyone in the world six times over. (T or F) **True**

WHAT do YOU KNOW?

Take the True and False Quiz below to see how well informed you are regarding environmental issues.

1. Experts say at the current consumption rates, the world's known oil reserves will be used up in 80 years. (T or F)

2. Burning fossil fuels is the main cause of the greenhouse effect or global warming. (T or F)

3. The world population has more than doubled since 1950. (T or F)

4. By the time an American reaches age 75, he or she will have produced 5 tons of garbage, used 6 million gallons of water, and used two times as much energy as the world average. (T or F)

5. Each of us is responsible for contributing to the greenhouse effect. (T or F)

6. Americans use an average of 100,000 aluminum cans every week. (T or F)

7. About 30 acres of the earth's forests are destroyed every minute. (T or F)

8. Every ton of recycled paper Americans buy saves 17 trees. (T or F)

9. It takes 500 recycled milk jugs to make a six-foot plastic park bench. (T or F)

10. Americans drive the distance to the planet Pluto and back every day. (T or F)

11. Each year, do-it-yourself oil changers improperly dump more oil than the oil that tanker Exxon Valdez spilled into Alaska's Prince William Sound. (T or F)

12. Every year Americans discard 1.1 million tons of disposable plates and cups. This is enough to set a picnic for everyone in the world six times over. (T or F)

BIBLICAL IMAGES: BREAD

© UMPH

SESSION 1: BREAD AS SACRED FOOD

SESSION 2: MANY GRAINS, ONE LOAF

Purpose:

This unit deals with the image of bread as it is used in the Bible, with particular emphasis on how this image can help us to better understand Jesus and why he is referred to as "the bread of life."

This Is Not Junk Mail!

IT'S IMPORTANT STUFF FROM YOUR TEENAGER'S SUNDAY MORNING LEADER

BREAD AS A SYMBOL

Ask your family what they think of when they smell bread baking. Think of some of the analogies used in the Bible to represent Jesus. Hopefully one that will come to mind is, "I am the bread of life." What do you think Jesus meant by that statement? Together, look up and read John 6:35. Is this a good analogy to describe Christ? Why or why not? What is your favorite analogy to describe Christ?

COMMUNION

Ask your family members what goes through their minds when they take Communion. How do they feel when they eat the bread and drink the grape juice? Do they know how Communion is taken in other Protestant churches? How do the Catholics take Communion? Perhaps your parents could ask some of their friends from other religions how their church celebrates Communion. How often do they take it? What do they use for the elements? Do they believe the elements are symbols or the actual body and blood of Christ? If they are uncomfortable asking their friends these questions, go to your local library and check out a book about other religions to find out the answers to the above questions.

BAKE BREAD ...BREAK BREAD

As a family, bake some bread together. If your family does not know how to bake bread from scratch, buy a loaf of frozen bread dough which can be found in your grocery store's frozen food section. After the bread is baked, enjoy eating it hot out of the oven. Think about the taste, smell and texture of fresh-baked bread. Or have your family offer to bake some bread for Communion one Sunday at your church. Another idea is to bake some bread and then deliver it to someone you know who is sick, home-bound, frazzled or lonely. Perhaps your family could find a soup kitchen in your area where you could help serve meals to homeless or hungry people. The food pantry in your area could probably use volunteers anytime to help them stock shelves or distribute food.

Hallelujah!

IDEAS FOR PEOPLE WHO PLAN WORSHIP

These ideas can be used in class to supplement the material. You can also copy this page and give it to your pastor or the Chair of Worship.

The following hymn suggestions can be found in many main-line denominational hymnals.

"For the Bread Which You Have Broken"
"I Come with Joy"
"One Bread, One Body"
"Fill My Cup, Lord"
"Let us Break Bread Together"

Prayer Suggestion: "Bread and Justice" by Rubem Alves

MAKE A COMMUNION BANNER

As a class, formulate plans for making a banner which could be used in your sanctuary on Communion Sundays. Some ideas for the banner could be to incorporate patterns of a loaf of bread, a chalice, grapes, a grapevine, a cross, or Jesus breaking bread. Use a large piece of felt or burlap for the background. Cut out the pictures and words from felt and then glue them down on the banner. Find someone with a sewing machine and have them sew a pocket into the top of the banner so that a dowel rod can be pushed through it. A cord can then be tied to each end of the dowel rod.

LOOK AT COMMUNION LITURGY

Examine some of the common Communion liturgies printed in the hymnal your church uses. Locate the one that your church uses most often on Communion Sunday. Next, decide if there is another one which you think your congregation should try. Ask your pastor or worship committee if this liturgy could be used the next time your congregation takes Communion. Tell them why you would like to try it; afterward, try to get some feedback from the congregation as to how they liked it.

HELP with COMMUNION

Arrange with your pastor to have some of the youth in your class help with Communion. Some members of the class could gather at someone's home and, with a parent's help, bake bread to be used in the Communion service.

Some other students could come to church early and help your Communion stewards set up Communion. Still others could actually help serve Communion. Make sure you set all of this up ahead of time with your pastor or worship committee.

Miscellany

IDEAS FOR TEACHERS

When all of your youth are in one class, you may want to make some adjustments to the lesson. Keep in mind that your younger youth may still be thinking of bread as a food item. It may take them longer to begin to think critically about Jesus as our "bread of life." If the class doesn't move along at a quick pace, your older teens may become bored since they are already doing quite a bit of abstract thinking at school. Break into groups at different times to allow the older youth to discuss a question on their own. Ideally, when you split the class into two groups, have another adult in the classroom who can facilitate the older group.

HITTING CLOSE TO HOME

Hunger is a sensitive issue. We take it for granted that all Americans have enough food each day on their tables to more than satisfy themselves. This, however, is not the case. You may live in an area where some families in your church really do not have enough to eat. Or perhaps your students go to school with children who are not getting enough food to eat.

Hopefully, you will know your class well enough before teaching this session that you will be aware of any class members who are in need of food. If this is not the case however, and someone brings to your attention that their family often goes hungry, you will want to confidentially relay this to your pastor or a social service agency that might help them. Be sensitive to their feelings.

PRODUCE SOME SKITS

If your older students seem to want to explore more with the sessions, invite them to write some brief skits and present them to the class or even to some younger classes. Some passages that deal with bread and would lend themselves well to a skit might be:

Luke 9:10-17
Feeding the 5000

Matthew 26:26-30
Last Supper

Matthew 4:1-11
Jesus being tempted by the devil

Exodus 16
The story of the manna in the wilderness

SESSION 1:

BREAD AS SACRED FOOD

FOCUS

To examine what bread is, how it is used in the Bible, and its significance as a Christian symbol.

SCRIPTURE

Deuteronomy 8:3

HERE'S THE PLAN | **DO IT YOUR WAY**

OPTIONS	TIME (minutes)	PREPARATION	SUPPLIES
INITIAL CONNECTION			
A Construct a Food Pyramid	10	get copy of food pyramid & make outline of food pyramid	chalk or markers
B Play Breadbasket Upset	10		chairs and space
CONNECT WITH THE SESSION			
A What Is Bread?	10	buy bread; cut small loaves of bread out of paper	napkins, bread, cut-outs
B The Bread Box	10	make copies of YouthPage	YouthPage, pencils
CONNECT WITH THE BIBLE AND THE FAITH COMMUNITY			
A Locate Scripture Passages About Bread	15		Bibles, white paper plates, and markers
B Play Bible Charades	20	prepare papers with five Scriptures	slips of paper with Bible passages written out on them.
C Hymn Search	15		hymnals, pencil, paper
D Bake Bread Together	20	talk to pastor and Communion stewards about youth making bread.	YouthPage, recipe, bread ingredients
CONNECT WITH LIFE			
CLOSING CONNECTION			
A Take Communion Together	15		juice & bread, hymnals, Bibles

Desired Result:
To loosen up the class before the lesson.
(Choose Option A or B.)

INITIAL CONNECTION

CONSTRUCT A FOOD PYRAMID

Outline of food pyramid, chalk or markers
(Allow 10 minutes.)

As students enter, direct them to the outline of the pyramid taped to the wall or drawn on a chalkboard. Challenge them to work as a group to try and construct the government food pyramid.

Ask them to fill in the different food category levels and note how many servings, according to the U.S. government, we should eat from it daily.

When everyone has arrived, show them the actual food pyramid and tell them that today's topic is bread.

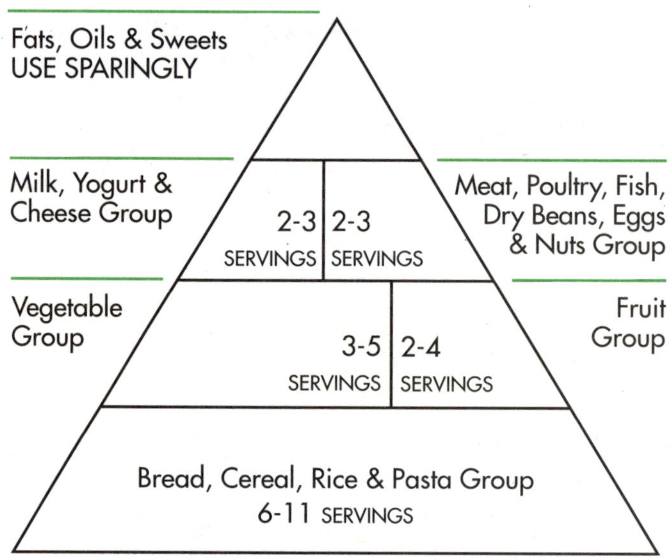

Source: U.S. Department of Agriculture

PLAY BREADBASKET UPSET

Chairs and space
(Allow 10 minutes.)

Push back your tables and have everyone sit on a chair in a circle. Have the class number off by fours. Call the ones "wonder bread," the twos "Italian bread," the threes "rolls" and the fours "bagels." Assign someone to be the caller in the center of the circle and remove their chair.

The caller yells out one of the types of breads from the list above. When they do this, everyone who was assigned that type of bread must change places with some other member of that group. While the changes are taking place, the caller tries to find an empty chair. If the caller succeeds, the person left without a place to sit becomes the caller. Whenever he or she wishes the caller may say "Breadbasket," which means everyone changes seats.

CONNECT WITH THE SESSION:

A WHAT IS BREAD?

Desired Result:
To begin thinking about what bread is.
(Choose Option A or B.)

Small loaves of bread cut out of paper and enough pieces of bread (store bought or homemade) for each class member, napkins
(Allow 10 minutes,)

Hand out a napkin and a piece of bread to each student and tell them to eat their piece of bread, or at least one bite. (Take up the leftovers to feed to the birds.)

After they have eaten the bread, give each person the paper bread and tell them to write down one word they think describes bread.

Then have them use tape to place their loaf on a chalkboard or wall.

Read through all of the adjectives aloud and **ASK:**

➤ **Where would we be without bread?**

➤ **Do you need bread in your diet to sustain your body?**

➤ **Is bread a new food? (Read brief history of bread from ReadMe.)**

B THE BREAD BOX

A copy of YouthPage for each student and a pencil
(Allow 10 minutes.)

S

Instruct your students to look at the questions on the YouthPage and jot down quick answers to each question. Then have them compare answers with a student sitting next to them.

Desired Result:
To begin examining what the Bible has to say about bread
(Choose Option A, B, C, or D.)

CONNECT WITH THE BIBLE AND FAITH COMMUNITY

A LOCATE SCRIPTURE PASSAGES ABOUT BREAD

Bibles, white paper plates, and markers
(Allow 15 minutes.)

S

SAY:

- **"Think for a moment about some of the stories in the Bible which deal with bread. Can anyone guess know how many times the word *bread* is written down in the Bible?" (300 times)**
- **Can you think of any stories or Bible passages that involve bread? List each reference on a paper plate. (After they have suggested all that they can think of, list a few more from the references on ReadMe.)**
- **In most of the Bible passages, do you think bread is more than just something to eat?**

B PLAY BIBLE CHARADES

Slips of paper with the following Bible passages written out on them: Exodus 16:1-8; Matthew 4:1-4; 26:26; Luke 9:10-17; 14:15-24
(Allow 20 minutes.)

S

Break the class into small groups of four or five students. If your class is small, have each person do this individually. Hand each group or person a slip of paper with a Scripture reference. Tell them to locate the passage and spend a few minutes figuring out how they could pantomine it.

Have each group or person give a pantomine and ask the rest of the class to guess what passage or story they are depicting.

C HYMN SEARCH

hymnals
(Allow 15 minutes.)

Break into small groups and assign each group a hymn which uses the word *bread* in it. (Use suggestions from the Hallelujah! page.) Ask the groups to read through the words and think about what the hymn says to us today. Do you like this hymn? If you were going to write a hymn about bread what might you say?

Be prepared to have each group say something about the hymn they selected.

D BAKE BREAD TOGETHER

bread ingredients, kitchen
(Allow 20 minutes.)

Before this session, ask the pastor if your class could provide the bread for Communion the next time it is served at your church. Move the class to your church kitchen. Let the youth take turns mixing the dough. If your class is large, mix up several different batches of dough, perhaps making leavened and unleavened. (Note: If you make yeast bread, you will have to take it home to bake it. Then put the finished loaves in your freezer.)

Make sure your church Communion stewards know that your class will be providing the bread for the next Communion Sunday. Put a small note in your church bulletin telling the congregation your class made the Communion bread.

CONNECT WITH LIFE

TAKE COMMUNION TOGETHER

A

Desired Result:
To explain Communion and help youth feel comfortable

hymnals, Bibles
(Allow 15 minutes.)

If your pastor is free during your Sunday school hour, ask him or her to come in and lead a brief Communion service for your class using one of the liturgies from the hymnal. If your pastor is not free, consider asking a retired pastor or ask your pastor to come in after your Sunday school hour.

After Communion has been taken, invite the class to ask your pastor any questions they might have regarding Communion. Ask your pastor to describe what it was like the first time he or she served Communion.

© JONATHAN A. MEYERS

CLOSING CONNECTION

Read aloud the prayer which is written at the top of the Read Me.

Tell the class to begin thinking about some ways in which they, as a class, might help to feed hungry people in the world or in your community. Tell them that next week the class will form an action plan for how they might do this.

© JONATHAN A. MEYERS

Desired Result:
To stimulate youth to begin thinking about ways in which they can help others who are hungry.

Read Me

THIS IS WHAT YOU NEED TO KNOW ABOUT THE TOPIC.

CENTERING PRAYER

O God,
We've wasted
We've complained
We've grumbled.
We've misused our resources
We've confused our needs
with our wants.
For these sins
Father, forgive us.
Help us
reset our priorities
according to Your will.
Amen.

From *The More-With-Less-Cookbook* by Doris Longacre (Herald Press, © 1976) page 8.

UNLEAVENED BREAD

Jewish people eat matzo, which is bread without yeast, or unleavened bread, to symbolically mark their eviction from Egypt. In Exodus 12:39 it says, "They baked unleavened cakes of the dough that they had brought out of Egypt; it was not leavened, because they were driven out of Egypt and could not wait, nor had they prepared any provisions for themselves." After the Exodus, leaven became the symbol of evil and selfishness. Fermentation was seen as a corruption of the dough, which could not be offered to God, and matzo became a reminder of their freedom. This is why at Passover the Jewish people still eat unleavened bread.

A BRIEF HISTORY OF BREAD

Evidence, found from wood-fired ovens in the Middle East, leads historians to speculate that bread was baked in them about 9,000 years ago. Early breads were made by mixing flour with water and baking the dough. This early bread would not be anything like the bread we eat today. To make bread light, you must use a leavening agent such as yeast or baking powder, which create bubbles of carbon dioxide that inflate the dough.

Archaeologists think that the first leavening came from airborne spores of yeast that landed onto wet dough as it was being mixed. The yeast spores began feeding on the dough and multiplying. This process is known as fermentation. Baking bread has changed little since ancient civilizations discovered this fermenting process.

SCRIPTURE RELATED TO THIS SESSION

Exodus 12:14-20, The first Passover is described.

Deuteronomy 8:3, An admonishment not to forget that we must "not live by bread alone, but by every word that comes from the mouth of the Lord."

Exodus 16, This entire chapter describes manna, or "bread from heaven."

Matthew 4:1-4, Describes Jesus' encounter with the devil tempting him to turn stones into bread.

Matthew 6:11 and Luke 11:3, The Lord's Prayer.

Luke 14:15-24, This passage begins with the words, "Blessed is the one who will eat bread in the kingdom of God!" And then leads into the parable of the great dinner.

John 6:22-34, Jesus tells a crowd about the true bread from heaven telling them, "the bread of God is that which comes down from heaven and gives life to the world."

John 6:35, Jesus continues to tell the crowd, "I am the bread of life. Whoever comes to me will never go hungry, and whoever believes in me will never be thirsty."

Matthew 26:26, Here Jesus shares the Last Supper with the disciples and tells them of the bread, "Take, eat; this is my body."

Matthew 13:33, Parable of the Yeast.

Luke 9:10-17, Story of Jesus feeding the 5000 and making the five loaves and two fish feed everyone.

THE TRADITION OF COMMUNION

Within the Christian church there is no act of worship which is so rich in meaning as the Sacrament of the Lord's Supper. Communion has its origins in the Last Supper which Jesus shared with his disciples before his death (1 Corinthians 11:23-25). When we receive the elements of bread and grape juice, we are remembering Jesus' body which was broken for us, and his blood which was shed for us. It is interesting to note that Jesus saw in the common things of life the symbol of the spiritual. When we partake of the bread and juice, we are symbolically accepting the mercy that God offers us through Christ's crucifixion and resurrection.

When we receive the elements of bread and grape juice, we are remembering Jesus' body which was broken for us, and his blood which was shed for us.

THE Bread BOX

1. Think about a time you were really hungry. How did it feel? Write down some adjectives to describe how you felt.

2. Have you ever smelled the fragrance of fresh-baked bread coming out of an oven? List some adjectives describing how you felt.

3. Make a quick list of as many different types of bread products as you can.

4. Do you think the United States uses our food resources wisely? Why or why not?

5. Do you think you or your family waste much food?

6. Do you think the U.S. uses the most grain per person or the least?

Recipe for Unleavened Bread:

1/2 cup shortening, packed well
2 Cups of flour
pinch of salt
small amount of sugar
water to mix to a stiff dough

Mix first four ingredients, adding only a little water at a time. Make small balls of dough and flatten between your palms. Put into a cake pan and bake for 10 minutes in a hot oven. Or heat a small amount of shortening in an electric skillet. Then place a small amount of dough, flattened, in a hot electric skillet. Cook each side quickly until light brown.

These are good with honey and should be eaten warm.

Hey! Copy this page for your youth—really, we want you to!

SESSION 2

MANY GRAINS...ONE LOAF

FOCUS:

To look at Jesus as our "bread of life," to examine Communion and to think about how we can help to feed our world both physically and spiritually.

SCRIPTURE:

John 6:35

HERE'S THE PLAN | **DO IT YOUR WAY**

OPTIONS	TIME (minutes)	PREPARATION	SUPPLIES
INITIAL CONNECTION			
A One Body—Equally Important	15	list bread ingredients on board or newsprint	pencils, index cards
CONNECT WITH THE SESSION			
A Bread in Communion	15	copy roles onto cards	two index cards with the roles written on them, newsprint
B Communion Jargon	10	make copies of YouthPage	YouthPage, pencils
CONNECT WITH THE BIBLE AND THE FAITH COMMUNITY			
A The Bread of Life	20	prepare paper strips	Bibles, white sheets of paper cut into 4" wide by 12" long strips, and colored markers
B Good Yeast	15		Bible, yeast, sugar, several cups of warm water
C Give Us This Day	5		
CONNECT WITH LIFE			
A World Hunger Action Plan	10		Bible, Read Me
CLOSING CONNECTION			
Helping Feed Others Spiritually	20	collect newspaper sections; make copies of YouthPage	several front page & metro sections of recent newspaper, scissors, YouthPage

AN INITIAL CONNECTION

ONE BODY—EQUALLY IMPORTANT

SAY:

➤ **I've listed on the board the different ingredients that make up bread:**

- **flour**
- **yeast**
- **water**
- **salt**
- **oil**

Each of these ingredients is necessary to make bread bake correctly. If one ingredient is left out, the bread will not come out properly. Next to each ingredient, I've placed a brief description of the ingredient (flour—trusty main ingredient, water—holds all together, yeast—agent which makes bread cells multiply, salt—just a pinch to interact with other ingredients, oil—keeps all ingredients mixing well).

NEXT:

➤ **Ask each student to choose an ingredient that they think represents themselves in the body of Christ.**

➤ **Then have the class break into groups according to what ingredient they chose. In the small groups, everyone should tell why they chose that ingredient**

(Example: *I think that I am like yeast because I am always inviting people to Sunday school and youth group to try and help our groups grow and multiply.*)

Desired Result:
To understand how we are all important members of Christ's body.

pencils, index cards
(Allow 15 minutes.)

S

Desired Result:
To examine the importance of bread in Communion.
(Choose Option A or B.)

Two index cards with the roles written on them, newsprint
(Allow 15 minutes)

S

CONNECT WITH THE SESSION

A BREAD IN COMMUNION

Randomly hand a role-play card to two volunteers. Cards should read:
CARD #1: You are to pretend to be someone who has never been to church and have never heard of Communion. Keep asking questions, arguing, and wondering why bread is used in it.

CARD #2: You are a lifelong Christian trying to explain what Communion is to someone who has never been to church or witnessed a Communion service. Use simple terms to explain it.

After the roleplay
SAY:
I've taped a graffiti board to the wall of our classroom. Take a marker and write on the wall what Communion means to you. Don't sign your name to this and be completely honest because we are not going to criticize any comments.

Copies of the YouthPage for each student and pencils
(Allow 10 minutes.)

S

B COMMUNION JARGON

Direct the class to the YouthPage. Ask them to fill out the "Staff of Life" section.

After everyone has finished, briefly go over their answers. (Answers can be found on Read Me, page 121.)

CONNECT WITH THE BIBLE:

THE BREAD OF LIFE

A

Desired Result:
To examine how Jesus is our "bread of life."
(Choose Option A, B, or C.)

Bibles, white sheets of paper cut into 4" wide by 12" long strips, and colored markers
(Allow 20 minutes.)

Begin by reading John 6:22-40 aloud to the class.

Ask the students what they think it means to say Jesus is "the bread of life." Give everyone a strip of paper and markers. Ask them to write down a bumper sticker slogan which would show others on the road why Jesus is their "bread of life."

Stick these up around the room as students finish, and ask for a few students to tell why they put down a particular slogan.

THE BREAD OF LIFE

B

Desired Result:
To understand how we can be "good yeast" in the world.

Bible, yeast, sugar, several cups of warm water
(Allow 15 minutes.)

S

Tell the class that they are going to conduct an experiment today. Give each student or group of students a cup of warm water. Tell them to put in a teaspoon of yeast and a pinch of sugar. (Do not stir.)

Next, have someone read Matthew 13:33 to the class. Talk about what a parable tries to do. (*It conveys a deep meaning through a simple story.*)

Look at the cups and ask someone to describe what is happening.

Who do you think Christ might be comparing the yeast to in the parable? (*Christians*)

According to this parable, are we to mix with others in the world? (*yes*)

If we do, what will happen? (*We might bring others to the kingdom of heaven. We can mix with others and Christ's love and possibly bring others to Christ, thereby multiplying the kingdom.*)

Desired Result:
To begin to think about our role in helping to alleviate world hunger.

(Allow 5 minutes.)

S

GIVE US THIS DAY

SAY:

- **Can you think of a line from the Lord's Prayer which mentions bread? (*"Give us this day our daily bread."*)**
- **What do you think this means for us as Christians?**
- **Why would Jesus include that in his model prayer?**
- **Do you think Jesus was speaking of spiritual bread or physical bread?**
- **What's the difference?**

Bible, Fact Sheet
(Allow 10 minutes.)

S

CONNECT WITH LIFE:

WORLD HUNGER ACTION PLAN

Ask a class member to read Luke 9:10-17. Afterward, ask the class if they think there is anything we can do to help those around the world who don't have enough food to eat. Read aloud facts regarding hunger found on Read Me.

- **Brainstorm a list of some of the ways your class might help to alleviate world hunger.**
- **Read to them some of the organizations that work toward alleviating world hunger.**
- **As a class, choose a project to launch to help alleviate hunger. (Sponsor a canned food drive or choose an organization that works toward alleviating hunger and raise money for it.)**

CLOSING CONNECTION

HELPING FEED OTHERS SPIRITUALLY

SAY:

- **We know that we can help alleviate the suffering of those who are hungry. We can also help those who are starved spiritually. I am closing today by handing out several sections from recent newspapers. Take a few moments to look through the section you are handed. Cut out an article that you think could use our prayers.**

- **When everyone has their prayer request ready, take the requests and then tape the article on a wall or bulletin board. After each request, as a class say, "Lord, hear our prayer."**

- **Remind the students that one way we can help to nourish others as well as ourselves is to have an active prayer life. By praying we keep an open communication with God. Jesus seems to stress that the most important thing about praying is keeping at it.**

Close by reading the litany on the YouthPage.

Desired Result:
To help students think about those around the world in need.

Several sections of recent newspapers and scissors (Probably front page sections—metro and national news sections are best.); copies of the YouthPage for each student
(Allow 20 minutes.)

Read Me

THIS IS WHAT YOU NEED TO KNOW ABOUT THE TOPIC.

SESSION 2 FACT SHEET

CENTERING PRAYER

Be gentle when you touch bread
Let it not lie uncared for, unwanted,
So often bread is taken for granted.
There is so much beauty in bread—
Beauty of sun and soil
Beauty of patient toil.
Winds and rains have caressed it;
Christ often blessed it,
Be gentle when you touch bread.

From *The More-With-Less-Cookbook* by Doris Longacre (Herald Press, © 1976) p. 59.

BREAD

When we break bread together we are acknowledging our dependence upon both food and upon each other. We cannot live by bread alone, but neither can we live without it. We need bread, the food, to keep our physical bodies alive. We need "the bread of life" to keep our spiritual life alive. When we sit down to eat a meal with others, to break bread together, we are engaging in fellowship with one another.

FEEDING THE WORLD

It is projected by some demographers that the world's population will double during the next half century going from 5.3 billion people in 1990 to more than 10 billion by 2050. Expert opinions vary as to whether the world will have enough food to feed all of these persons. Some say the growing population is a catastrophe in the making and that farmers will have to intensify agricultural practices in order to grow enough grain to feed all the world's inhabitants. Other experts fear a massive famine is in the making. The result of famine is mass starvation. At the present time it is predicted that about 1 billion people worldwide are malnourished because they do not have enough food.

IDEAS FOR HELPING TO SHARE OUR BREAD

Perhaps after talking about bread and it's properties which make it a very necessary part of life, your class may want to reach out to those who do not have much bread. There are many organizations dedicated to alleviating world hunger.

UNITED METHODIST COMMITTEE ON RELIEF (UMCOR)

This organization, which was begun in 1940, ministers to persons in need all over the world. You can order resources through: The Service Center, General Board of Global Ministries, 7820 Reading Road, Caller No. 1800, Cincinnati, Ohio 45222-1800.

HEIFER PROJECT INTERNATIONAL (HPI)

The HPI was begun in 1944 and assists persons in 37 countries and 12 states to alleviate hunger by providing livestock and training so families can feed themselves as well as others. For more information about their projects, contact: Heifer Project International, World Headquarters, 1015 South Louisiana, Little Rock, AR 72202 (800)-422- 0472.

CHURCH WORLD SERVICE (CWS)

This ecumenical group established in 1946 works through the National Council of Churches to help persons in more than seventy countries. One of their well-known programs is the CROP walk. You may obtain information by contacting: Church World Service, P.O. Box 968, Elkhart, IN 46515 (219)-264-3102.

ANSWERS TO YOUTHPAGE QUESTIONS: STAFF OF LIFE QUIZ

1. Why is bread used when we take Communion? • **Bread is used because it represents Christ's body being broken for us.**

2. Why do you think bread is such a fitting symbol for Jesus to use for a Communion element? • **Bread is a common everyday food item. We consider bread to be a staple in our diets, something we cannot live without. (Just as we can not really live without Christ in our lives.)**

3. During the Passover celebration, Jewish people eat unleavened bread. What ingredient is left out to make it unleavened? • **Yeast**

4. In many Christian churches, Communion is also called:
   1) Eucharist 2) Lord's Supper 3) Mass 4) All • **All of the above**

5. True or False? Unleavened bread was first made in the Ancient Near East and Egypt about 2600 B.C. • **False. Unleavened bread was first made in the Ancient Near East and Egypt thousands of years earlier.**

6. What crisscross-shaped bread treats were created in 610 A.D. by Italian monks who gave them to children as a reward for learning their prayers? • **Pretzels**

7. Which of these foods can be used for making bread?
   1) potatoes 2) ground acorns and beech nuts 3) bananas 4) All • **All of the above**

8. What breakfast bread—made of flour (symbolizing the staff of life), milk—(symbolizing innocence), and egg—(symbolizing rebirth), became a popular food as part of Christians' annual Lenten observance? • **Pancakes**

YOUTHPAGE

Staff OF Life Quiz

BREAD LITANY

Leader: "Give us this day our daily bread."
People: Lord, we pray for those who do not have bread to eat today, we ask that you would be with them. Give them bread to eat.
Leader: "You shall not live by bread alone."
People: As well as physical food we also need your spiritual food. Lord, feed us and nurture us in your word so that we may grow strong in the faith.
Leader: "I was hungry and you gave me food. I was thirsty and you gave me drink."
People: We do not know hunger as do many of our neighbors around the world. Help us not to waste food and take it for granted.
Leader: "Taking the five loaves and the two fish he looked up to heaven, and blessed, and broke them and gave the loaves to the disciples, and the disciples gave them to the crowds."
People: God of love, help us to share our food so that it might stretch around the world.
Leader: "The Lord Jesus on the night when he was betrayed took bread, when He had given thanks, He broke it, and said, 'This is my body which is broken for you.'"
People: When we eat we experience fellowship with one another and fellowship with you. Help us to remember that eating is a blessing and food a gift.
Leader: "He was known to them in the breaking of the Bread."
People: Let us break bread together.
All: Amen!

1. Why is bread used when we take Communion?

2. Why do you think bread is such a fitting symbol for Jesus to use for a Communion element?

3. During the Passover celebration, Jewish people eat unleavened bread. What ingredient is left out to make it unleavened?

4. In many Christian churches, Communion is also called:
   1) Eucharist 2) Lord's Supper 3) Mass 4) All

5. True or False? Unleavened bread was first made in the Ancient Near East and Egypt about 2600 B.C.

6. What crisscross-shaped bread treats were created in 610 A.D. by Italian monks who gave them to children as a reward for learning their prayers?

7. Which of these foods can be used for making bread?
   1) potatoes 2) ground acorns and beech nuts
   3) bananas 4) All

8. What breakfast bread—made of flour (symbolizing the staff of life), milk—(symbolizing innocence), and egg—(symbolizing rebirth), became a popular food as part of Christians' annual Lenten observance?

A NEW LOOK AT OLD FRIENDS

© CLEO PHOTOGRAPHY

SESSION 1: "THEN GOD SPOKE . . . .A NEW LOOK AT THE TEN COMMANDMENTS"

SESSION 2: "THE LORD IS MY SHEPHERD . . . A NEW LOOK AT THE TWENTY-THIRD PSALM"

SESSION 3: "FOR GOD SO LOVED . . . A NEW LOOK AT JOHN 3:16"

PURPOSE:

To connect with familiar Bible texts in order that youth might experience God's saving love and respond to God's call to enter into loving relationships with God and neighbor.

This Is Not Junk Mail!

IT'S IMPORTANT STUFF FROM YOUR TEENAGER'S SUNDAY MORNING LEADER

THEME TALK - LIFE IS BUSY! TALK ABOUT THE BIBLE!

As family life becomes increasingly busy, parents tend to rely solely on the church for the religious education and the spiritual growth of their youth. Families, however, exert a very powerful influence on young persons. What better place to ask questions and learn about the nature of God than within the safety and love of one's own family? Set aside a regular time to talk about issues in the Bible.

This unit takes a new look at the Ten Commandments in Exodus 20:1-17 and the Great Commandment in Matthew 22:34-40. It explores the idea of God as a shepherd who cares for us, provides for us, and protects us, as presented in Psalm 23. Finally, it examines God's gift of love and spiritual rebirth through Jesus Christ and the joys of believing in Christ, as presented in John 3:16.

FAITH FOCUS - MEMORIZE SCRIPTURES TOGETHER — FOR FUN!

When you were young, did you memorize the Ten Commandments, the Great Commandment, Psalm 23, or John 3:16? If you did not, consider doing so now. Engage your own family in the process. You might want to make the memorization a fun part of a traditional family event. Your own involvement in trying to learn the Scriptures "by heart" can be a source of joy and delight for your youth. Use the memorization of Scriptures in a lighthearted way to build bridges between you and your youth and to add to the sense of family unity. Celebrate one another's successes and support one another's struggles. Avoid making the project mandatory. Keep it fun!

TALK · ABOUT · RULES!

Each family has some sort of set expectations of one another. Families operate by rules that may be clearly agreed upon or that may be just understood. Families benefit by talking about rules and expectations.

Begin by evaluating where you are. What rules are in place? Why do you have them? What purposes do they serve? What are the underlying principles of your family rules? The Ten Commandments and the Great Commandment are based on the principles of love for God, self, and neighbor. How might these principles influence your family rules?

Think about what you want to have happen as a result of having and following family rules. Which of your family rules would you change? What rules would you eliminate? What rules would you add?

If family rules lead to a deeper respect and love for God and for one another, you can be assured that they are good!

the Golden Rule

"In everything do to others as you would have them do to you; for this is the law and the prophets."

Matthew 7:12

Hallelujah!

IDEAS FOR PEOPLE WHO PLAN WORSHIP

IDEAS for PEOPLE WHO PLAN WORSHIP

Consider having the youth lead Sunday morning worship. Several of the activities in this unit can be adapted for use in congregational worship. Look at the following:

"Then God Spoke . . ." skits (2A), interview with Moses and Jesus (3A), to do list (3C), group prayer (5). "The Lord is My Shepherd . . ." Praise God name game (1C), pantomime of Psalm 23 (3A), Scripture choir (3C). "For God So Loved . . ." skit (3B), imagine John 3:2-17 (3C), play (4C), worship (5)

Also, check your hymnal, book of prayer, or book of worship for songs, responsive readings, and litanies that are appropriate. For the session on the Ten Commandments, check under index topics such as "Christian Perfection," "Discipleship and Service," and "Guidance."

Check under "Providence" in the index and look up hymns such as "The Lord Is My Shepherd, I'll Not Want," and "The King of Love My Shepherd Is."

Practice the motions for the body prayer illustrated on the next page, and present this to the congregation as the focal point for the opening or closing of worship.

A BODY PRAYER OF THE GREAT COMMANDMENT

Love
(Cross hands over heart.)

the Lord Your God
(Hands move up with palms out; touch together over head; hands flow back down to sides.)

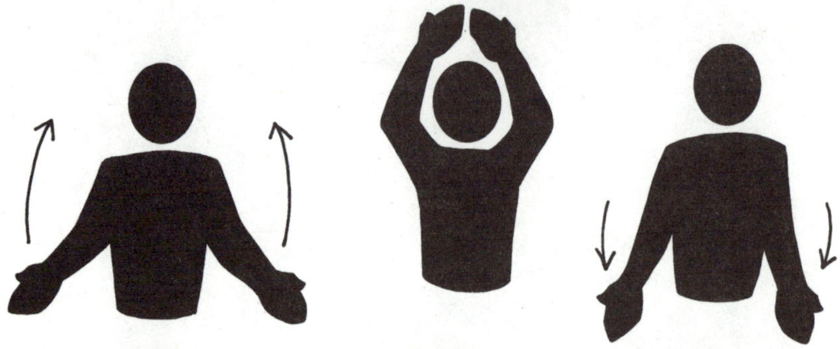

with all your heart, soul, and mind,
(Cross hands over heart. Thrust arms out and up slightly, then move hands up to stroke across forehead.)

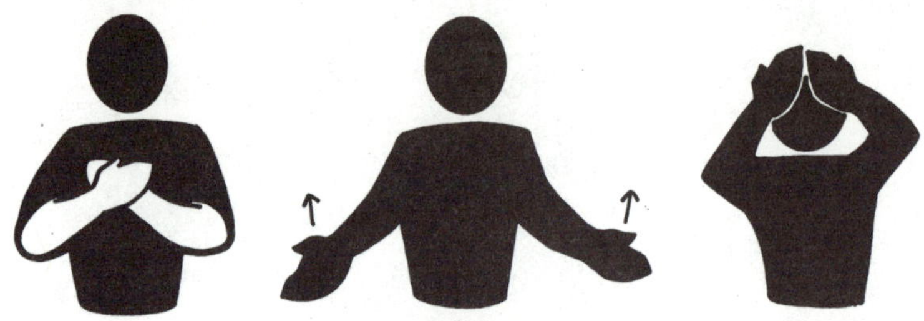

and love your neighbor
(Hands reach out in front of body.)

as you love yourself.
(Wrap arms around body in a hug.

ILLUSTRATION BY SUSAN HARRISON

Miscellany

IDEAS FOR TEACHERS

When All the Youth Are in One Class

Most youth who have grown up in the church have had to memorize or study the Scriptures in this unit. While memorizing Scriptures can make them so familiar that a person may overlook their deeper meanings, memorization has many benefits. In a time of need, a Bible verse may be a source of strength or comfort. Memorization is an effective way to apprehend the key ideas of a loving, supporting God. A memorized verse reveals layers of truth over years of physical, spiritual, emotional, and intellectual growth. If the youth in your group have not memorized any of the Scriptures in this unit, challenge them to do so. The Great Commandment and John 3:16 are fairly easy to memorize. Since they are longer, offer some special reward, a class party for example, for memorizing the Ten Commandments or Psalm 23 .

The familiar Scriptures of this unit invite youth of all ages to look at the love and providence of God; to consider the heart of religious rules or laws and how they affect relationships with all people of all ages, races, and cultures and to explore God's gifts of new life and love through Jesus Christ. The heartbeat of Psalm 23, the Ten Commandments, the Great Commandment, and John 3:16, is the steadfast love and care of God for all creation. Our own capacity to love flows from the heart of God's love.

> In a time of need, a Bible verse may be a source of strength or comfort.

If all the youth in your church are in the same class, you can point out the values of listening to and showing respect for youth of different ages. Each age group will have different ideas about similar topics and life experiences. Such diversity can stimulate healthy discussion. Youth who are learning how to listen to and show respect for one another even when their ideas are different will be more open to learning new ideas.

When youth of different ages are in one class, some may feel too shy to speak. Have youth sit in circles. Pose a question and have each youth in the circle respond in turn. Be sure to ask questions that they can't "miss." Ask their feelings or opinions. Accept all their responses.

Session 3, Activity 4C describes the creation of a play in which a youth encounters God's love and experiences spiritual rebirth. You may want to expand this activity over two or three sessions and have them prepare the play for a church dinner, another class, or for the entire congregation.

SESSION 1:

THEN GOD SPOKE:

A NEW LOOK AT GOD'S COMMANDMENTS

FOCUS:

To explore the Ten Commandments and the Great Commandment as the principles of thought, feeling, and action that lead to growth and wholeness.

SCRIPTURE:

Exodus 20:1-17; Matthew 22:34-40

HERE'S THE PLAN | DO IT YOUR WAY

OPTIONS	TIME (minutes)	PREPARATION	SUPPLIES
INITIAL CONNECTION			
A Treasure Hunt	10	prepare clues and Ten Commandments tablet	cardboard, small pieces of paper, tape
B Play "Commandments"	10	create gameboard	roll of butcher paper, markers, one die from a pair of dice
CONNECT WITH THE SESSION			
A Create Skits	10-12		
B Create a Community	8-10		
CONNECT WITH THE BIBLE AND FAITH COMMUNITY			
A Interview Moses and Jesus	10	make copies of YouthPage	YouthPage, Read Me, Bibles
B Talk Show	10	make copies of YouthPage	YouthPage, Read Me, Bibles
C "To Do" Lists	10	make copies of YouthPage	paper, pencil, YouthPage, Read Me, Bibles
CONNECT WITH LIFE			
A Have A Discussion	10	make copies of YouthPage, small pieces of paper	basket, chalkboard and chalk or large white paper and markers
B TV Program Guide	10		paper and pencils
C Write a Story	10	make copies of YouthPage	chalkboard and chalk or large sheet of white paper and markers, paper and pencil
CLOSING CONNECTION			
A Create Group Prayer	5		

INITIAL CONNECTION

A TREASURE HUNT

A

Desired Result:
To connect with one another and the theme of God's law.
(Choose Option A or B.)

cardboard, small pieces of paper, tape
(Allow 10 minutes.)

Ahead of time make a "stone tablet" of the Ten Commandments by cutting the tablet from a piece of cardboard and writing the Ten Commandments on the tablet or by using pages 136 and 137. Make some signs to designate the following scenes from the story of the Exodus: Egypt; the Red Sea; heaven; rock; Mt. Sinai. Tape the above signs to different parts of the learning area. Write the following clues on small pieces of paper:

a. God delivers the people from bondage in Egypt (Exodus 7-12).
b. God divides the waters of the Red Sea (Exodus 14).
c. God provides manna from heaven (Exodus 16).
d. God provides water from the rock (Exodus 17).
e. God gives a great treasure at Mt. Sinai (Exodus 19-20).

Hide clue "b" near the sign that says **Egypt**. Hide clue "c" near the sign that says **Red Sea**. Hide clue "d" near the sign that says **Heaven**. Hide clue "e" near the sign that says **Rock**. Hide the **stone tablets** of the Ten Commandments near the sign that says **Mt. Sinai**.

Tell the youth a great treasure is hidden in the wilderness. They must find the treasure. Read aloud clue "a." Tell them to use clue "a" to find the next clue. Follow all the clues to the treasure.

B COMMANDMENTS

large sheets of paper, markers, one die from a pair of dice
(Allow 10 minutes.)

Ahead of time create a life sized board game as follows:

Draw lines across a large sheet of paper to create squares large enough to stand in. Make twenty-one squares. Write JOY in the last square. Write the brief forms of the Ten Commandments on ten of the squares. Write the following sentences in some of the empty squares:

➤ **"OOOPS! You broke one! Move back a space!"**

➤ **"OOOPS! You broke more than one! Move back three spaces!"**

➤ **"You listened to God's will! Move forward three spaces!"**

➤ **"You showed great respect for your parents. Move forward two spaces!"**

Tape this game board to the floor.

SAY:

➤ **God's family is harmonious, happy, and full of the potential for growth. Your goal for the game is to participate in God's family by following God's instructions which will lead you to JOY.**

Have the youth take turns throwing the die and moving forward the number of squares indicated on the die. They must follow any directions written on the square they land on. The first youth to get to the "JOY" square is the winner.

(Choose Option A or B.)

CONNECT WITH THE SESSION

CREATE SKITS

A

(Allow 10-12 minutes.)

S

ASK:

➤ **What rules in your life annoy you?**

➤ **Which rules do you wish were different?**

➤ **What rules in your life make you feel secure?**

Have the youth develop three short skits (1-2 minutes) of the following topics. If your group is large, have them form three teams and give one of the skit assignments to each team.

a. Life in a town with no rules.
b. Life in a town with too many rules.
c. Life in a town with rules based upon love of God and neighbor.

In the skit, have the youth pretend that a group of people are going to the movies. They must travel across town to get to the movies.

Have the youth present the skits.

ASK:

➤ **In what ways do rules affect the lives of the people in this community?**

➤ **In what ways might rules be good for the community? bad for the community?**

➤ **What do you think rules should be based on in order to be of most benefit to the community?**

CREATE A COMMUNITY

B

paper, pencils
(Allow 8-10 minutes.)

S

Have the youth form groups of two or three. Tell them to discuss what makes an ideal community. They are to decide who lives in it, where it is located, what the people do, and what the rules of the community should be.

Tell them to write the rules of the community. When they have finished, ask them to tell briefly about their community and read the community's rules.

ASK:

- ➤ **Do you agree with the rules of this ideal community? Why or why not?**
- ➤ **What rules would you add? What rules would you leave out?**
- ➤ **How does life lived in relationship with God affect the life of your ideal community?**

CONNECT WITH THE BIBLE AND THE FAITH COMMUNITY

Desired Result:
To explore the Ten Commandments and the Great Commandment
(Choose Option A, B, or C.)

INTERVIEW MOSES AND JESUS

A

YouthPage, Fact Sheet, Bible
(Allow 10 minutes.)

S

Have the youth read aloud the Ten Commandments and the Great Commandment from the YouthPage. Have them look at Exodus 20:1-17 and Matthew 22:34-40. Tell in your own words the information about the commandments written on ReadMe.

SAY:

- ➤ **God's commandments are more than just rules. They are divine principles for living in the peace and joy God intends for all creation.**

Choose youth to play the roles of Moses, Jesus, and a team of news reporters. Have the news reporters ask questions of Moses and Jesus about the commandments.

HAVE A TALK SHOW

B

YouthPage, Read Me, Bibles
(Allow 10 minutes.)

S

Have the youth read aloud the Ten Commandments and the Great Commandment from the YouthPage. Tell in your own words the information about the commandments from "Bible Background" on ReadMe.

Choose a youth to play the role of a talk show host. The remaining youth will be the studio audience. Have the talk show host ask:

➤ **What do these commandments tell us about our relationship with God?**

➤ **What do these commandments tell us about our relationship with ourselves?**

➤ **What do these commandments tell us about our relationship with our neighbors?**

Youth will take turns going to the "mike" to suggest responses to the questions.

paper, pencil, YouthPage, Bible Background, Bibles ***(Allow 10 minutes.)***

C MAKE "TO DO" LISTS

Have the youth look over the Ten Commandments and the Great Commandment on the YouthPage. Have them look at the commandments as written in Exodus 20:1-17, and Matthew 22:34:40. Tell in your own words the background information on Read Me.

Have the youth form two teams. Give one team the Ten Commandments and the other team the Great Commandment. Have the Ten Commandments group rewrite the commandments as a "to do" list. Have the Great Commandment team create a "to do" list based on the Great Commandment.

Have the teams present their "to do" lists when they have finished.

ASK:

➤ **How are the "to do" lists alike?**

➤ **How are the "to do" lists different?**

➤ **What do these lists say to you about the connection between love of God, self and neighbor, and one's actions?**

(Choose Option A, B, or C.)

CONNECT WITH LIFE

small pieces of paper, basket, chalkboard and chalk or large white paper and markers ***(Allow 10 minutes.)***

S

A HAVE A DISCUSSION

Write the following words on small pieces of paper, one word to each piece of paper: *home, school, businesses, the mall, the movies, TV, radio, music, sports, the environment, cities.* Fold these and place them in a basket. Write the following question on a chalkboard or large sheet of white paper: What would the world be like if everyone followed the Ten Commandments? Have the youth think about the question.

Tell them they are going to discuss how different things in our world would be if everyone in our culture followed the Ten Commandments. Have the youth sit in a circle. Have one person take a small piece of paper from the basket and read the word, and tell what his or her experience of the word might be like if everyone followed the Ten Commandments. Have the next youth in the circle take a piece of paper from the bowl and repeat the process. Continue until all the pieces of paper have been discussed.

B MAKE A TV PROGRAM GUIDE

paper and pencil
(Allow 10 minutes.)

S

Have the youth imagine what one day's TV programs would be like if everyone on earth followed the Ten Commandments. Tell them to create a TV program guide with a brief description of programs for one day. Start the programs at 6 AM. Have them list other programs throughout the day until midnight.

C WRITE A STORY

chalkboard and chalk or large sheet of paper and markers, paper and pencil
(Allow 10 minutes.)

S

Write the following plot line on a chalkboard or large sheet of white paper.

1) Someone is experiencing difficulty.
2) They find a ancient scroll with the Ten Commandments and the Great Commandment written on it. (The ancient scroll might be the YouthPage.)
3) The scroll changes things.

Have the youth create stories based on the plot. Have them answer the following questions to get started:

➤ **Where and when does your story happen?**

➤ **Who is the person who finds the scroll?**

➤ **How does finding the scroll change things?**

Have the youth read or tell their stories when they finish.

CLOSING CONNECTION

(Allow 5 minutes.)

S

CREATE A GROUP PRAYER.

Have the youth pray a group prayer as follows:

EVERYONE: LOVE THE LORD YOUR GOD WITH ALL YOUR HEART, ALL YOUR SOUL, AND ALL YOUR MIND.

Have the youth pray silently about ways to love God. Tell them to say aloud a word or sentence that names a way to love God as they feel moved to pray. If no one says anything, simply pray silently.

EVERYONE: LOVE YOUR NEIGHBOR AS YOU LOVE YOURSELF.

Again, have the youth pray silently and respond with a word or sentence that names a way to love neighbor or self as they feel moved to pray.

Close with the following:
"Thank you God, for your gracious gift of divine guidance, and for teaching us how to treat you, ourselves, and one another; in Christ we pray. Amen."

Read Me

THIS IS WHAT YOU NEED TO KNOW ABOUT THE TOPIC.

PREPARING YOURSELF

Preparing to bring youth into an encounter with God's Word in Scripture provides you, as their teacher, an opportunity to grow spiritually. Find a special place and have your Bible, paper, and pen handy. Begin by opening yourself to God's guidance.

What do rules and laws mean to you?

How do you respond to them?

Do they help you feel secure?

Do you rebel against them?

Read Exodus 20:1-17 and Matthew 22:34-40. Read the Bible Background below. What basic insights do you gain about God from these commandments? What do you think God intends for human relationships? How might these commandments apply to your relationships?

Look at the Connect with Life Activities. What do you think daily life would be like if everyone on earth followed the Ten Commandments and the Great Commandment?

Pray for your youth and for yourself as follows: "God of all good gifts, thank you for giving us boundaries of human behavior based on love and respect for you, for ourselves, and for others. Guide me as I lead the youth. Help them feel a deeper desire to do your will; in Christ I pray. Amen."

BIBLE BACKGROUND

The Ten Commandments and the Great Commandment may be thought of as the underlying principles of the more specific laws or codes of behavior written in the Scriptures. Like a heartbeat, they send life to all the other laws given by God so that the people might experience harmony, growth, and wholeness.

The Ten Commandments: The Ten Commandments found in Exodus 20:1-17 and in Deuteronomy 5:6-21 summarize the law or Torah spelled out in Exodus, Leviticus, Numbers, and Deuteronomy. The Hebrew term Torah, which originally meant instruction, came to mean a way of life for the faithful community of Israel. It is both story and law because it includes the story of God's saving activity in the midst of the people. God and the people of Israel entered into a covenant agreement at Mount Sinai, and this covenant is the foundation for God's gift of the law. God saved the people from bondage in Egypt, and because of God's action, the people were called to worship only God and to obey God's laws.

The Ten Commandments are not arbitrary rules. They are principles of conduct toward God and toward one another that, when followed, will bless the people with harmony, growth, and wholeness.

The first three commandments specify the principles of relationship with God. The people are called to worship only God, to avoid making images of God, and to avoid wrong use of God's name. Making an image or idol tends to limit God to one of God's attributes. The Hebrew people understood that God's nature is beyond full representation by the human mind. God is more than anyone is able to imagine. The Hebrews understood that the use of God's name in magical ways for personal desires was not only inappropriate, but impossible as well. God is beyond human manipulation or control. God is to be approached with love, gratitude, and a willingness to do God's will. The positive command to remember the Sabbath day and keep it holy recognizes the need for rest, devotion, and reflection upon God's saving grace. The remaining commandments set the boundaries for behaviors among God's people in order to enhance community growth, harmony, and wholeness. The commands call for respect of persons and their property.

The tenth commandment instructs the people to avoid the act of coveting that which belongs to another. To covet is to desire or want something. It signifies an inner attitude which may well take shape as an action and points to the inner spirit as the place where wrong action begins. Jesus echoed this commandment when he said "First clean the inside of the cup, so that the outside also may become clean" (Matthew 23:26) and "For out of the heart come evil intentions, murder, adultery, fornication, theft, false witness, slander. These are what defile a person, . . ." (Matthew 15:19-20).

The Great Commandment: In the same way that the Ten Commandments distill the Covenant Code to the basic principles of behavior underlying the code, the Great Commandment of Jesus further distills the commandments to three loves—God, self, and neighbor. The Great Commandment is found in three of the gospels: Matthew 22:34-40; Mark 12:28-34; and Luke 10:25-28. In Matthew's gospel the scribe asks which commandment is the greatest in order to test Jesus. Jesus responds by quoting Deuteronomy 6:5 and Leviticus 19:18, the two principles underlying all the law.

THE TEN COMMANDMENTS

—You shall have no other gods before me.

—You shall not make for yourself an idol.

—You shall not make wrongful use of the name of the Lord your God.

—Remember the Sabbath day and keep it holy.

—Honor your father and your mother.

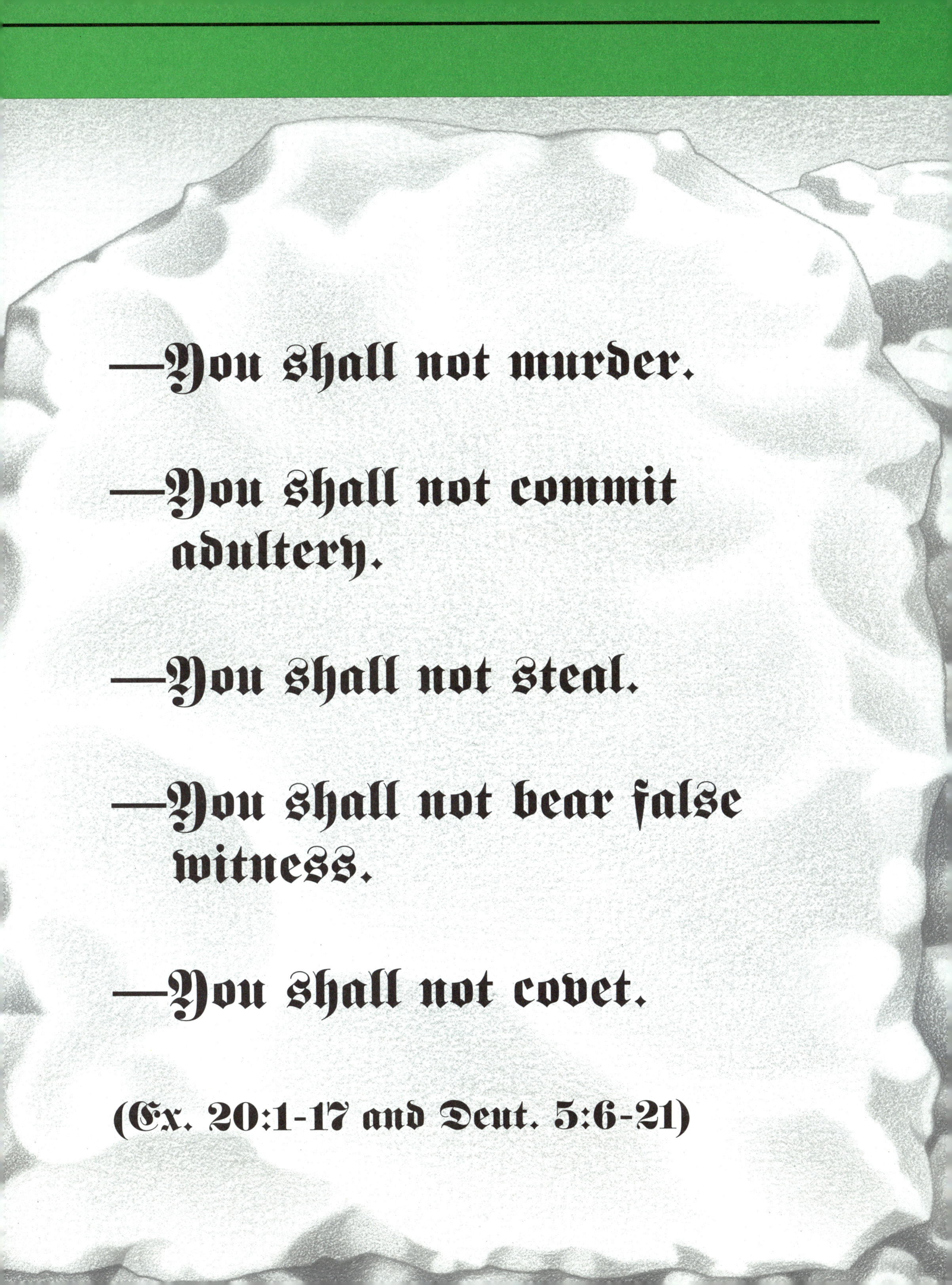

—You shall not murder.

—You shall not commit adultery.

—You shall not steal.

—You shall not bear false witness.

—You shall not covet.

(Ex. 20:1-17 and Deut. 5:6-21)

YOUTHPAGE

Grace, COVENANT, & Law

The law or "Torah" is more than just a system of rules. It is a way of life for God's people that grew out of the covenant between God and the people of Israel. The covenant was based on what God had already done for the people by saving them from bondage in Egypt. The response to God's saving grace was to worship only God and obey God's law. God's law was given as a good gift which would insure harmony, growth, and wholeness among God's people. Both the Ten Commandments and the Great Commandment summarize the basic principles of the law.

THE GREAT Commandment

" 'You shall love the Lord your God with all your heart, and with all your soul, and with all your mind.' This is the greatest and first commandment. And a second is like it: 'You shall love your neighbor as yourself.' On these two commandments hang all the law and the prophets" (Matthew 22:37-40).

"What's coveting?"

—Do you really like something that belongs to someone else?
—Do you want it for your own?
—Are you thinking about a way you might get it whether they want you to have it or not?
Well, that's coveting!

THE 10 COMMANDMENTS

- You shall have no other gods before me.
- You shall not make for yourself an idol.
- You shall not make wrongful use of the name of the Lord your God.
- Remember the Sabbath day and keep it holy.
- Honor your father and your mother.
- You shall not murder.
- You shall not commit adultery.
- You shall not steal.
- You shall not bear false witness.
- You shall not covet.

(Exodus 20:1-17 and Deuteronomy 5:6-21)

SESSION 2:
FOR GOD SO LOVED. . . A NEW LOOK AT JOHN 3:16

FOCUS:

To explore what it means to believe in God's great gift of love through Christ and to explore ways such belief leads to personal and communal renewal.

SCRIPTURE:

John 3:16

HERE'S THE PLAN | **DO IT YOUR WAY**

OPTIONS	TIME (minutes)	PREPARATION	SUPPLIES
INITIAL CONNECTION			
A "I Just Love" Discussion	8		stopwatch or watch w/second hand
B Play "We believe It!"	8		
CONNECT WITH THE SESSION			
A John 3:16 Video Game	10		Bible, paper and markers
B John 3:16	10		Bibles, chalkboard and chalk or large white paper and markers
CONNECT WITH THE BIBLE AND THE FAITH COMMUNITY			
A Write in Nicodemus' Diary	10	make copies of YouthPage	paper, pencil, Bible, YouthPage, Read Me
B Create Skits	10	make copies of YouthPage	Bible, YouthPage, Read Me
C Imagine Events in John 3:2-17	10	make copies of YouthPage	Bible, Read Me, YouthPage
CONNECT WITH LIFE			
A Create a Poster	10	make copies of YouthPage	YouthPage, Read Me, poster paper
B Create a Comic Book	10-15	make copies of YouthPage	YouthPage, 8 ½" x 14" paper, markers
C Create and Perform a Play	15	make copies of YouthPage	YouthPage, Read Me, Bibles
CLOSING CONNECTION			
Worship Together	5	make copies of YouthPage	YouthPage, small table, candle, candle holder, matches, Bible

Desired Result:
To connect with one another and with the word "love"
(Choose Option A or B.)

(Allow 10 minutes.)
a stopwatch or watch with second hand

S

INITIAL CONNECTION

A HAVE AN "I JUST LOVE___" DISCUSSION

Have the youth form two circles, one inside the other; the inside circle faces out, and the outside circle faces in. Each youth should face a partner.

Tell youth they must spend a total of thirty seconds talking with their partner about a food they just love. Time the conversation with a watch. At the end of thirty seconds say "Stop. Inside circle move one person to the left." When the inside circle has moved one person to the left, tell the youth to spend thirty seconds talking about a movie they just love. Repeat the process for each topic below.

movie star
sport
athlete
school subject
music
musician
TV show
TV star
car

Desired Result:
To explore the meaning of John 3:16.

(Allow 8-10 minutes.)

S

B PLAY "WE BELIEVE IT"

Have the youth form two teams. Tell the youth on each team to think of a story about themselves that is either true or untrue to tell to the group. They will tell their group and the class leader whether it is true or untrue.

Each team will take turns telling one of their stories to the other team. They must convince the other them that each story is true, whether it is or not.

Have one team choose a youth to tell their story. The other team must decide whether the story is true or untrue. If they decide it is true, they say in unison, "We believe it." If the story is untrue, they say in unison, "We doubt it." If they guess correctly, they get a point. If they guess incorrectly, the other team gets a point. Continue play until everyone has had an opportunity to tell a story. The team with the most points wins.

CONNECT WITH THE SESSION

A CREATE A JOHN 3:16 VIDEO GAME

Desired Result:
To explore the encounter between Jesus and Nicodemus.
(Choose Option A or B.)

Bible, paper and markers
(Allow 10 minutes.)

S

ASK:

➤ **"Who can say from memory John 3:16?"**

Begin reciting the verse. Invite the youth to say it with you. Have the youth locate John 3:16 in their Bibles. Have a youth read John 3:16-17 aloud.

ASK:

➤ **What does John 3:16-17, say to you about God?**

➤ **Have the youth tell about their favorite video game.**

ASK:

➤ **What happens in each level or world of your video game?**

➤ **What would happen with the video game characters if the game were based on John 3:16?**

Have the youth use paper and markers to draw a video game with two or three levels using John 3:16 as the basic principle for the actions of the video game characters. When they have finished, have them explain what they have drawn.

B WRITE AND PERFORM A RAP VERSION OF JOHN 3:16

Desired Result:
To explore the relationships between John 3:16, spiritual rebirth, and life choices.

Bibles, chalkboard and chalk, or large white paper and markers
(Allow 10 minutes.)

Have a youth read aloud John 3:16.
SAY:

➤ **God loves the world. God wants some things in our world to change. What things?**

Write their responses on the chalkboard or a large sheet of white paper.

SAY:

➤ **God offers new life through Jesus Christ. John 3:16 calls for belief in Christ. When people believe, what might happen with each thing you listed?**

Write their responses on the chalkboard or large white paper.

Have the youth write and perform a rap version of John 3:16 using the Bible verse and the two lists.

Desired Result: To offer thanks for God's love and to make a commitment to a specific loving action. **(Choose Option A, B, or C.)**

CONNECT WITH THE BIBLE AND THE FAITH COMMUNITY

A WRITE A PAGE IN NICODEMUS' DIARY

paper, pencil, Bible, YouthPage, Read Me ***(Allow 10 minutes.)***

S

ASK:

➤ **What does the word "believe" mean to you?**

Write responses on a chalkboard or large white paper.

Have a youth read aloud the paragraph entitled "Believing—More than Saying 'It's True.'" Tell in your own words the information on Bible Background entitled "Loving and Believing."

Read aloud the story of the encounter between Nicodemus and Jesus in John 3:1-21. Tell the class the information about Nicodemus from Read Me.

Have the youth imagine that Nicodemus goes home and writes in his diary about the conversation he has had with Jesus. What would he write? When the youth have finished, have them read what they have written.

B CREATE SKITS

Bible, YouthPage, Read Me, chalkboard & chalk, or paper and markers ***(Allow 10 minutes.)***

S

ASK:

➤ **What does the word *believe* mean to you?**

Write responses on a chalkboard or large white paper.

Have a youth read aloud the paragraph from YouthPage entitled "Believing—More than Saying 'It's true.'" Tell in your own words the information from Read Me entitled "Loving and Believing."

Have the youth imagine that Nicodemus goes to the home of a close friend after his conversation with Jesus. He tells his friend about the conversation and expresses his feelings or thoughts about it.

ASK:

➤ **What does Nicodemus say to his friend?**

➤ **How does Nicodemus' friend respond to the story?**

Have the youth form teams of two or three and prepare short skits about Nicodemus and his friend.

After the skits ASK:

➤ **Do you feel the same or different from Nicodemus? his friend? explain.**

IMAGINE THE EVENTS IN JOHN 3:2-17

Bible, Read Me, YouthPage, chalkboard & chalk, or paper and markers
(Allow 10 minutes.)

ASK:

➤ **What does the word *believe* mean to you?**

Write responses on a chalkboard or large white paper.

Have a youth read aloud the paragraph entitled "Believing—More than Saying 'It's True.'" Tell in your own words the information from Read Me entitled "Loving and Believing."

Have the youth relax and close their eyes. Tell them to imagine that it is night and the streets are quite dark. A man is walking cautiously through the streets. They follow him. The man sees Jesus and speaks to him. Read aloud John 3:2-17. Be silent for a few seconds.

SAY:

➤ **Imagine that Nicodemus has left. Jesus sees you and smiles. Imagine that Jesus explains to you about the conversation with Nicodemus. What does Jesus say to you?**

Allow a few seconds of silence.
SAY:

➤ **Tell Jesus "Thank you." Become aware of this room. When you are ready, open your eyes.**

ASK:

➤ **What was the feeling of walking through the dark streets?**

➤ **What did you feel as you followed Nicodemus through the streets to Jesus?**

➤ **What do you think Nicodemus was feeling during the conversation?**

➤ **What do you think Jesus was feeling during the conversation?**

➤ **What do you think happened with Nicodemus after this conversation with Jesus?**

➤ **What did you learn from your conversation with Jesus?**

Desired Result:
To explore and explain the imagery of the Scripture.
(Choose Option A, B, or C.)

CONNECT WITH LIFE

A CREATE A POSTER

YouthPage, Read Me, poster paper
(Allow 10 minutes.)

S

Before class, cut out a large cloud from a sheet of white poster paper. Write "Born From Above" across the cloud.

Have a youth read aloud John 3:3.

ASK:

➤ **What do you think Jesus means when he says "born from above?"**

Write responses on the cloud around the phrase "born from above."

Have a youth read aloud the paragraph beginning "Born from above? What does that mean?" from the YouthPage. Tell in your own words or read the information from Bible Background, entitled "Born from above."

Have the class members read to themselves the listing of places where spiritual rebirth can make a difference. Ask them to respond to the questions by sharing their answers with the group. The situations can be ones that they have observed, been involved in, or imagine.

B CREATE A COMIC BOOK

YouthPage, 8 1/2" x 14" paper, markers
(Allow 10-15 minutes.)

Read aloud John 3:16.

ASK:

➤ **What difference does it make that God loves the world?**

Read aloud John 3:3. Have a youth read aloud the paragraph beginning "Born from above? What does that mean?" on the YouthPage. Tell in your own words or read the information from Bible Background entitled "Born from Above." Have the youth look at the list of different places on the YouthPage of school, home, and so forth.

ASK:

➤ **What difference does it make in all these places that God offers spiritual rebirth and life through Christ?**

Have the youth imagine a story about a person whose life is changed because of John 3:16. Tell them to make a comic book of their story using the paper and markers. They will fold the paper lengthwise to make the comic book. When they have finished, have them read or tell about their comic books.

CREATE AND PERFORM A PLAY

YouthPage, Read Me, Bibles
(Allow 15 minutes.)

C

Have a youth read aloud the paragraph beginning "Born from above? What does that mean?" on the YouthPage. Tell in your own words or read the information from Bible Background, entitled "Born from Above." Have the youth look at the list of different places on the YouthPage representing school, home, and so forth, and discuss answers to the question, "What difference can spiritual rebirth make in each of these places?"

Invite the group to work together to create a youth by agreeing on responses for the following:

➤ **What does the youth look like?**

➤ **What kind of personality does the youth have?**

➤ **What does the youth do at school?**

➤ **Does the youth work? If so, where?**

➤ **What kind of family life does the youth have?**

After they have created the youth,
SAY:

This youth needs to know and to believe God's love and to experience spiritual rebirth.

Tell the youth to make up a play with three scenes as follows:
Scene 1 - What is happening before the youth experiences God's love?
Scene 2 - How the youth experiences God's love.
Scene 3 - What happens in the life of the youth after the experience of God's love?

Have the youth present the play.

YouthPage, small table, candle, candle holder, matches, Bible
(Allow 5 minutes.)

CLOSING CONNECTION

WORSHIP TOGETHER.

Ahead of time, create an altar by placing a cloth over a small table. Place the candle in the candle holder and put it on the altar. Place the Bible on the altar.

Have the youth gather near the altar and light the candle. Have a youth read aloud John 3:16. Tell the youth to each write his or her name in the blank provided in the paraphrase of John 3:16 on the YouthPage. Have the group read the paraphrase together, each one saying his or her name as the group reads aloud.

SAY:
God's love calls for our response. What is one way in the week ahead you can show someone God's love?

Have them write a response in the open-ended sentence on the YouthPage. Close the session with the following prayer:

> **"God of all love and God of all life, thank you for the gift of eternal life and spiritual rebirth through Jesus. Help us to grow in our understanding of your great love for us; in Christ we pray. Amen."**

Read Me

THIS IS WHAT YOU NEED TO KNOW ABOUT THE TOPIC.

PREPARING • YOURSELF

Can you recite John 3:16 from memory? If you cannot, take time now to memorize it. Think about what the verse says to you. Write a summary of what it means.

John 3:16 gives the essence of God's attitude toward creation and God's work through Jesus. God's intent for creation is good. Think about your daily world for a moment. What needs to be healed? What needs to be made whole? What do you think God wants changed?

Read John 3:1-20. Read the Bible Background material on the next page. Imagine John 3:2-17 as described in Option 3C. Respond to the questions in the activity. What insights did you gain?

Look at the Closing Connection and do the activity for yourself. What does it feel like to say John 3:16 with your name?

Pray the following prayer: Lover of All Creation, thank you for loving me. Thank you for giving me an opportunity to lead the youth to a greater understanding of your love through the activities of this session. Guide me and help me to listen to them and to show them that you care for them; in Christ I pray. Amen.

BIBLE BACKGROUND

Nicodemus

John 3:16 occurs in Jesus' response to Nicodemus, a pharisee, a teacher of Israel, and a leader of the Jews. In John's gospel, Nicodemus questions Jesus (John 3), defends him (7:50–52), and participates with Joseph of Arimethea in his burial (19:38-42). Nicodemus has come to Jesus at night to engage in conversation. He addresses Jesus respectfully as "rabbi" or "teacher" and states the belief that Jesus has come from God because of the signs he has been doing (3:2). Jesus tells Nicodemus "No one can see the kingdom of God without being born from above." Nicodemus does not understand because he takes Jesus literally (3:4). Jesus continues explaining about spiritual rebirth and eternal life which one receives as one believes in the Son of Man (3:15).

Born from Above

Christians understand "being born from above" as spiritual rebirth or regeneration which may be thought of as the spiritual change in which God brings a person from a condition of spiritual defeat and death to a renewed condition of holiness and life. John 3:16 summarizes and emphasizes this work and motive of God in and through Christ. Because God loves, God gives spiritual rebirth and life. "For God so loved the world that he gave his only Son, so that everyone who believes in him may not perish but may have eternal life." John 3:17 further clarifies God's work: "Indeed, God did not send the Son into the world to condemn the world, but in order that the world might be saved through him."

Loving and Believing

The power of John 3:16 radiates through the verbs that express God's actions and human response. God "loved" and "gave" and those who "believe" will receive. The word *believe,* which occurs 136 times in the New Testament, occurs fifty-two times in John's gospel. It is translated from the Greek word *pisteuo* (pist–yoo'–o). The word includes a number of ideas in addition to agreeing that something is true. It means to have faith in, to commit oneself to, or to trust a person or thing. In John 3:16, to believe in Christ is to trust one's spiritual well-being to Christ. The English word *believe* comes from the old English word family for "leave" in the sense of granting permission. The word *love* comes from the same family! In English as well as in Greek, believing contains the sense of giving oneself in trust to another. To believe in Christ is to give oneself in trust to the love of God and God's gifts of spiritual regeneration and eternal life.

John 3:16 - For Everyone, Including You.

"For God so loved the world that he gave his only Son, so that everyone who believes in him may not perish but may have eternal life."

"For God so loved____that God gave you the only Son, so that if you believe, you may not perish but may have eternal life."

This week I can show God's love by ____________________________.

BELIEVING—More Than Saying "It's True."

The word *believe* means more than saying you think something is true. To believe is to give permission, to trust, to commit oneself, and to love!

"Very truly, I tell you, no one can see the kingdom of God without being born from above" (John 3:3).

Born from above? What does that mean? Nicodemus had difficulty understanding what Jesus meant. One aspect of spiritual rebirth, the gift that comes when we believe in Christ, means growing in our understanding of God's love and in ways we can grow in our love of God, self, and neighbor.

What difference can spiritual rebirth make:

at home?
in a class at school?
with your friends?
at the mall?
at a ball game?
at a school dance?

SESSION 3:

THE LORD IS MY SHEPHERD

FOCUS:

To explore God as One who loves, protects, and provides.

SCRIPTURE:

Psalm 23

HERE'S THE PLAN | DO IT YOUR WAY

OPTIONS	TIME (minutes)	PREPARATION	SUPPLIES
INITIAL CONNECTION			
A Play A Praise God Name Game	10		
B Have A Praise God Relay Race	10		masking tape or chalk
CONNECT WITH THE SESSION			
A Do A Mad Lib	10	make copies of YouthPage	paper, pencils, YouthPage
B Make Wallpaper	10	copy Psalm 23 on paper in one continuous line	large sheets of paper, markers
CONNECT WITH THE BIBLE AND THE FAITH COMMUNITY			
A Do A Pantomime of Psalm 23	5-8	make copies of YouthPage	YouthPage, Bibles
B Make an Investigative Report of Other Biblical References to Shepherds	10		Bibles
C Have a Scripture Choir	10		Bibles
CONNECT WITH LIFE			
A Create Collages	12-15		three sheets of poster paper, old magazines, markers, glue, scissors
B Create a God's House Poster	10	cut poster paper into shape of house	sheet of poster paper, mark-ers.
C Prepare A "Banquet"	10		modeling clay of different colors
CLOSING CONNECTION			
Create a Group Version of the Twenty-third Psalm	8	make copies of YouthPage	YouthPage, poster paper, markers

INITIAL CONNECTION

A PLAY A PRAISE GOD NAME GAME

Desired Result:
To break the ice and connect with one another.
(Choose Option A or B.)

(Allow 10 minutes.)

S

Have the youth sit in a circle. Tell the youth to think of a quality they like about God. The quality must begin with the same letter as their name. Tell them to listen to the following sentence, put their name in the first blank and the quality they like about God in the second blank. "I ____ sing a song of praise for God's ______." For a youth with the name Pam, the sentence might read "I, Pam, sing a song of praise for God's power." Give the youth a moment to think of how they will complete the sentence. Begin the game by saying the sentence. Have the youth on your left say **their** sentence, then repeat **your** sentence. Have the next youth on the left say their sentence and the two preceding sentences. Each youth must remember all the sentences that come before his or her sentence. Play continues all the way around the circle. The last person must repeat ALL the preceding sentences.

B HAVE A PRAISE GOD RELAY RACE

Desired Result:
To experience the 23rd Psalm in new ways.

(Allow 10 minutes.)

S

Tell youth to place their name in the first blank and a quality about God that begins with the same letter as their name in the second blank of the following sentence:

"I, ____ sing a song of praise for God's _____.

Have the youth form two teams. Use chalk or masking tape to make two X's. To run the relay race each youth must run to his or her team's X, stand on the X, chant the sentence, then run back to tag the next person on the team. Chant the sentence by singing all the words on the same note except the quality about God. Sing that word on a higher note.

For example: "I, Pam, sing a song of praise for God's POWER."
The first team to finish the relay race wins.

Desired Result:
To explore today's images of God's guidance, protection, and provision and what they mean as we do God's work in our world.
(Choose Activity A or B.)

CONNECT WITH THE SESSION

DO A MAD LIB

A

paper, pencils, YouthPage
(Allow 10 minutes.)

S

Have the youth number from 1 to 17 on the paper. Have them write responses as directed in the following list:

1. A noun that names God in a special way for you
2. A verb that tells what will not occur because God is with you
3. A peaceful place where you experience God's presence
4. Another peaceful place where you experience God's presence
5. A verb that describes something God does
6. A word or group of words that tell where God leads you
7. A verb that tells how to get from one place to another
8. A scary place
9. Something scary
10. A noun that names something comforting
11. A noun that names something comforting
12. Your favorite meal
13. Something you do that keeps you from being your best
14. Your favorite cologne
15. Something good that God gives to you
16 Something good that God gives to you
17. A place where you would love to live all your life

Give each youth a copy of the YouthPage. Have them read the Twenty-third Psalm, placing their responses in the corresponding blanks.

MAKE WALLPAPER

B

large sheets of paper, markers
(Allow 10 minutes.)

Ahead of time, write the Twenty–third Psalm in one long continuous line on the paper. Tape this to a wall, or place it on a long table so that all the youth can write or draw on it. Tell the youth to illustrate this Psalm by writing or drawing below the words.

When the youth have completed the wallpaper, invite each one to tell about what he or she has written or drawn.

CONNECT WITH THE BIBLE AND THE FAITH COMMUNITY

Desired Result:
To explore the experience of God's guidance, protection, and provision as presented in the image of the shepherd.
(Choose Option A, B, or C.)

A PSALM 23 PANTOMIME

YouthPage, Bibles
(Allow 5-8 minutes.)

S

Read (any background material about shepherds) from Read Me. Read about shepherds from the YouthPage.

Have the youth prepare a pantomime reading of the Twenty-third Psalm as follows:

-one or more youth read the Psalm aloud
-remaining youth pantomime the parts as they hear them
-act out lying down in green pastures, being led by still waters, having a meal, being anointed with oil, and so forth

You may want to arrange with the pastor or with another group in the church for the youth to perform their pantomime.

B MAKE AN INVESTIGATIVE REPORT OF OTHER BIBLICAL REFERENCES TO SHEPHERDS.

Bibles
(Allow 10 minutes.)

S

Divide the youth into teams. Give each team one or more of the following Bible sources: Ezekiel 34:11-16; Matthew 18:12-14; Luke 15:3-7; John 10:7-18; John 21:15-17; Hebrews 13:20; 1 Peter 5:1-4.

Tell them to imagine they are investigative reporters. They should investigate what each passage says about shepherds and sheep.

ASK:

➤ **How does the passage use the image of a shepherd?**

➤ **What does the shepherd image say about God?**

➤ **What does the shepherd image say about God's work in our world?**

➤ **How does the image of the shepherd speak to you about what you need to do for God in our world?**

Have each investigative team prepare a news report about their passages for the whole group.

Bibles
(Allow 10 minutes.)

SCRIPTURE CHOIR

Have the youth do a Scripture choir reading of Psalm 23 as follows:

Several youth repeat softly:
"The Lord is my shepherd. The Lord is my shepherd.
The Lord is my shepherd. The Lord is my shepherd."

The effect will be that of a steady rhythm throughout. They will continue to repeat this phrase as:

The following voices chime in . . .

Youth 1 "The Lord is my shepherd"

Youth 2 "I shall not want"

Youth 3 "He makes me lie down in green pastures."

Youth 4 "He leads me beside still waters."

Youth 1 "He restores my soul."

Youth 2 "He leads me in paths of righteousness for his name's sake.

Youth 3 "Even though I walk through dark valleys I will fear no evil."

Youth 4 "For you are with me.

Youth 1 "Your rod and staff comfort me.

Change the repeated phrase to "Goodness and Mercy, Goodness and Mercy." *Several youth will repeat this throughout the remaining lines of the Psalm.*

Youth 2 "You prepare a table before me in the presence of my enemies."

Youth 3 "You anoint my head with oil."

Youth 4 "My cup overflows."

Youth 1 "Surely goodness and mercy shall follow me all the days of my life."

All the youth: "And I shall dwell in the house of the Lord my whole life long!"

CONNECT WITH LIFE

(Choose Option A, B, or C.)

A CREATE COLLAGES

three sheets of poster paper, old magazines, markers, glue, scissors.
(Allow 12-15 minutes.)

SAY:

➤ **The psalmist used the image of a shepherd to help people understand God's guidance, protection, and provision. The shepherd may not be as familiar to us today. Think about images from today's world that might suggest God's guidance, protection, and provision.**

Have the youth form three teams. Have the first team find pictures in the old magazines that suggest guidance. Have the second team find pictures that suggest protection. Have the third team find pictures that suggest provision. Tell the teams to use the pictures, poster paper, and markers to create a collage.

When the collages are finished, have each team tell how the selected images demonstrate guidance, protection, or provision.

B CREATE A GOD'S HOUSE POSTER

sheet of poster paper, markers
(Allow 10 minutes.)

Ahead of time, cut out a simple house shape from the poster paper. Make it large enough for all the youth to write or draw inside.

Have a youth read aloud the last stanza of the Twenty-third Psalm.

ASK:

➤ **What does it mean to dwell in God's house one's whole life?**

Invite youth to imagine a house in which they would live all their life with God. Have them imagine what it looks like; what furniture, if any, is in the house; and where it is located. Have the youth write about or draw their house on the God's house poster. When they are finished with the God's house poster, have them tell about what they have written or drawn.

ASK:

➤ **How many houses do you think will fit inside God's house?**

➤ **How many people live in God's house?**

➤ **What does the God's house poster suggest to you about those who live in God's house their whole life long?**

➤ **If you live with others in God's house who are different from you, how do you think you should treat the other residents?**

modeling clay of different colors.
(Allow 10 minutes.)

➤ **What can you do to make God's house a place of goodness and mercy?**

➤ **What can our class do? our church?**

PREPARE A "BANQUET"

C

Have the youth create a banquet using the modeling clay. Tell them to create modeling clay versions of their favorite food. Place their creations on a tray or on a small table to suggest a banquet.

Have a youth read aloud verse five of the Twenty-third Psalm.

ASK:

➤ **If God were preparing a special meal for you, what would it be?**

➤ **How would you feel if God prepared such a meal for you?**

➤ **What would a meal for a friend be? another youth in your group? a stranger?**

➤ **How big would God's banquet have to be in order to provide food for all God's people?**

➤ **In what ways can you help provide food for others? What can your class do?**

➤ **What can your church do?**

YouthPage, poster paper and markers
(Allow 8 minutes.)

S

CLOSING CONNECTION

CREATE A GROUP VERSION OF THE TWENTY-THIRD PSALM.

Read aloud Psalm 23 from the Bible. Have everyone in your group who has memorized the psalm say it in unison.

Write a group version of Psalm 23 by having the youth offer suggestions for the blanks in the Twenty-third Psalm on the YouthPage. Write their version on the poster paper.

Close the session by reading the group version of the Twenty-third Psalm together.

Read Me

THIS IS WHAT YOU NEED TO KNOW ABOUT THE TOPIC.

Prepare Yourself

How do you experience God?

What image comes to mind when you think about God?

The primary image in Psalm 23 is the shepherd. Read the Psalm and the Bible Background material below.

How does Psalm 23 add to your understanding of God?

Psalm 23 is often memorized. Memorization of Scripture takes time and energy, but it is a process well-worth the time and energy one uses. Memorization deepens the connection between Scripture and one's mind and heart, especially if the passages memorized have significant meaning to a person. If you have not already memorized Psalm 23, take some time to do so.

Look over the "mad lib" on the YouthPage. Think about how you would fill in the blanks. What images would suggest God's guidance, protection, and provision?

Pray: Guiding, protecting, and providing God, please open my mind and heart to experiencing you more deeply. Help me guide the youth I teach to a fuller appreciation of you as we explore Psalm 23 together; in the love of Christ, our good shepherd. Amen.

BIBLE Background

A shepherd is one who tends sheep, which were economically and religiously valuable to the people of biblical times. They were used for food, clothing, and religious sacrifice. Shepherding was a primary occupation and was very familiar to those who would sing Psalm 23. A shepherd led the sheep to food and water, then herded them back into their fold at night, protected them from wild animals, and counted to make sure none were lost. The shepherd guided the sheep with a long staff and used a shorter, more blunt rod to ward off animals that threatened them. A shepherd wore a heavy cloak for protection from the elements, carried a bag for food, and often played melodies on a reed flute for entertainment as well as to calm the sheep.

WORD STUDY

A word study of some of the Hebrew words used in Psalm 23 greatly enriches the images of God's guidance, protection, and provision. The Hebrew word for shepherd means to feed and to make friends with, in addition to describing one who tends sheep. God's guidance, protection, and provision combine with God's friendship. This idea is further enhanced by a look at the Hebrew words translated "goodness" and "mercy." The Hebrew word translated "goodness" includes such diverse ideas as beauty, joy, gratitude, value, bounty or prosperity, and kindness. Goodness is combined with mercy, the translation for the Hebrew word *chesed* which carries in its history the sense of bowing. The all-powerful God bows graciously to favor the psalmist with kindness and mercy.

The Hebrew word translated "goodness" includes such diverse ideas as beauty, joy, gratitude, value, bounty or prosperity, and kindness.

In addition to the image of God as shepherd, Psalm 23 offers the images of a banquet and anointing. These gracious acts of hospitality go beyond the mere provisions of hospitality so necessary for survival in near eastern culture. Such hospitality gives honor to the one who receives it. When added to the image of God as shepherd, these images further deepen the understanding of God's favor toward humankind.

OTHER SCRIPTURAL PASSAGES

Like Psalm 23, Ezekiel 34:11-16 describes God as a shepherd who cares for the sheep. Many other psalms and prophets use the figure of speech in a similar way. In the New Testament, shepherd imagery is used in parables and teachings and to describe Jesus. John 10:7-18 recalls Jesus' use of "good shepherd" who knows the sheep and lays down his life for them. John 21 describes Jesus' call for Peter to feed His sheep. Matthew 18:12–14 and Luke 15:3–7 record the parable of the lost sheep which expresses God's love. Hebrews 13:20 refers to Jesus as "the great shepherd of the sheep." 1 Pet. 5:1-4 compares the elders of the church to shepherds with Jesus as the chief shepherd.

A Provider & A Friend

A shepherd is one who takes care of sheep. The word also means feeding and being a friend. All of these meanings are important to the image of God as Shepherd in Psalm 23.

SHEPHERDS

Sheep had great economic and religious value to the people of biblical times. They provided food and clothing, and they were used for religious sacrifices. Being a shepherd was a common job that was very familiar to the people.

The job required leading the sheep to food and water, making sure none of them wandered away, were stolen, or were harmed by wild animals, then leading them back into the fold at night. It was a tedious and often dangerous job. A shepherd wore a heavy cloak for protection against the weather, carried a bag for food, used a staff to guide the sheep and ward off wild animals, and often played a flute for entertainment and to calm the sheep.

The Lord is my (1)____________. I shall not (2)___________.
He makes me lie down in (3)_______________.
He leads me beside (4)_________________.
He (5)________________ my soul.
He leads me in (6)_________________ for his name's sake.
Even though I (7)_________ through (8) _______________
I fear no (9)_______________ for you are with me.
Your (10)_________ and your (11)_____________ they comfort me.
You prepare a (12)_________________ before me in the presence of my (13)_________________.
You anoint my head with (14)_________________. My cup overflows.
Surely (15)______________ and (16)__________________ shall follow me all the days of my life.
And I shall dwell in (17)_______________ of the Lord my whole life long.

Who Are These Young People?

They are wonderful.
They are scary.
They have a particular outlook on the world.
They are adventuresome.
They are cautious.
They try on styles of behaving and dressing.
They want to be independent but, in spite of what they say, they need their parents more than ever.
Most of all, they are special.
They will never be this age again.

We ought to be thoughtful, informed, supportive. We ought to make the most of this time—for them and for ourselves.

They are Middle Schoolers!

© ESBIN-ANDERSON

By Nancy Berla, Anne T. Henderson, and William Kerewsky, from *The Middle School Years—A Parent's Handbook,* prepared by